Drop Dumplin's and Pan-Fried Memories...
Along the Mississippi

By Angie Thompson Holtzhouser

Edited by Margi Hemingway

Illustrations by Lee Ann Halstead

Published by FAYJOE Enterprises

COVER ART: The Gallery Etc., 302 Powell, New Madrid, MO 63869

To order additional copies of this book, use the order form in back of book, or if you would like to see **DROP DUMPLIN'S and PAN-FRIED MEMORIES** at stores in your area, please write for additional information:

FAYJOE Enterprises
P. O. Box 10
Lilbourn, MO 63862

ISBN 0-9658142-0-3
Library of Congress Catalog Card Number 97-90465

First Printing   August 1997   5,000 books
Second Printing   December 1997 3,000 books

Printed in the United States of America
TOOF COOKBOOK DIVISION

STARR★TOOF

670 South Cooper Street
Memphis, TN 38104

MANY THANKS

I want to thank my husband, Larry Joe, for never complaining and always having an encouraging word during the writing of this book; my little granddaughter, Ellie, for being the inspiration that turned a dream into a reality; Mother, Daddy, Rick and Johnna, for being my best cheerleaders; Joe and Margi, for sharing their secrets of success with me; Donna and Carolyn for never running out of good ideas; Pam, Kathleen and Marian for seeing that I never fell behind at my office; Lee Ann for the cover art; Laverne and Shirley, whose rendition of "That little old ant who thinks he can move a rubber tree plant, because he has high hopes," never stopped running through my head; and my sponsors-- who believed in my high hopes -- Casino Aztar-Diamonds Restaurant; Forty Carrots; Lambert's Cafe; Memphis Queen Line; Patricia's Tea Room & Gift Shop; River Birch Mall; Rosie's Bar & Grille; Royal N'Orleans; The Blue Owl Restaurant; and Wicker's Original Barbecue Marinade & Baste.

INTRODUCTION

Welcome to **DROP DUMPLIN'S AND PAN-FRIED MEMORIES ... Along the Mississippi.** Many of the family recipes and anecdotes in this cookbook have been handed down through six generations, while others are my own invention, or have been shared by friends and well-known folks along the Mississippi. I genuinely hope that you will enjoy cooking from this book as much as I have enjoyed creating it!

Most sincerely,

Angie J. Holtzhouser

THE RICHARDS IN ANGIE'S HEART

Richard Floyd Thompson - Grandfather
In loving memory
April 1, 1905   ---   June 18, 1971

Richard Lanois Thompson - "My Daddy"
October 3, 1925

Richard Eugene Mays - Uncle
June 10, 1949

David Richard Shutt - Cousin
In loving memory
September 19, 1953   ---   December 12, 1954

Richard Kevin Potter - "My Son"
August 27, 1972

Richard Allan Mays - Cousin
November 25, 1980

DEDICATION

This book is dedicated to my Mother and Daddy, **Richard** and **Tessie Thompson**, who have nurtured four generations at their kitchen table. It is at this table that every joy of life has been celebrated and that every mishap has been soothed by a bountiful feast prepared with love and served with understanding.

Richard and **Tessie Thompson**
Twenty-Fifth Wedding Anniversary
September 17, 1975

Irish Blessing

May the wind always be to your back, and

May the road always rise to meet you, and

May you be dead and in heaven a half-hour,

before the devil knows that you are dead.

LARRY JOE HOLTZHOUSER is my husband and my buddy. Our life is like a hot fudge sundae. Even when it melts a little, it's still good!

Larry Joe and **Angie**

I am proud to say that **RICHARD KEVIN POTTER** is my son. Rick's quick wit and hot peppery nature always make life interesting. He is my best achievement, and he is Ellie Potter's daddy!

JOHNNA FOURTHMAN POTTER is my daughter-in-law. She is quiet and gentle like warm baked bread. Along with being Rick's wife, she is Ellie Potter's mommy and my friend.

Rick and **Johnna** putting on the Ritz!

ELLIE POTTER, my beloved little granddaughter, has now taken her place at the kitchen table adding extra sprinkles of joy to our food and to our lives. At seventeen months with a twinkle in her brown eyes, she asks for a bite of everything that you are eating by saying, "Hum!, Hum!" It works every time.

Ellie, age 17 months, 1997

ROBIN HOLTZHOUSER and I love the same man very much -- my husband and her father-- Larry Joe Holtzhouser. Like popcorn and butter, Robin and I are a likeable combination.

Robin, age 3, 1965

"TUDE" and "TOOTIE" HOLTZHOUSER are fun-loving and endearing in-laws. They gave me the "apple-of-my-eye," Larry Joe Holtzhouser.

"Tootie," Larry Joe and **"Tude"** in 1944

In loving memory of "Tude" Holtzhouser
March 8, 1921 - April 25, 1997

Notes

TABLE OF CONTENTS

Angie's Cousins - In Loving Memory

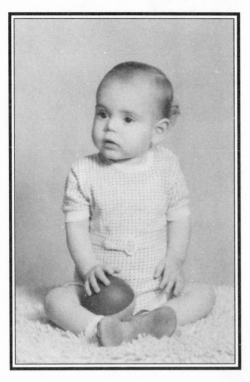

Charlie Ronald Shutt
August 22, 1950-
September 2, 1951

David Richard Shutt
September 19, 1953-
December 12, 1954

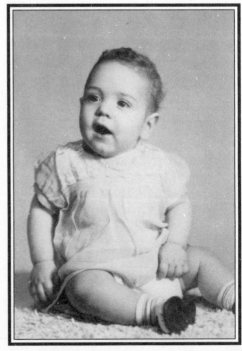

RECIPES AND MEMORIES FROM THE HEART

EASTER WITH PAPPY AND THE LEPRECHAUN

SUCCULENT BABY-BACK RIBS

ONION FRIED POTATOES

RUBEN'S FANCY IRISH SODA BREAD

IRISH MARMALADE BREAD PUDDING

KNIGHT OF THE ROUND TABLE

HUMMINGBIRD CAKE & CREAM CHEESE FROSTING

MAKING MUSIC ON SATURDAY NIGHT

AUNT LOU'S CRAZY CRUST PIE

DROP DONUTS

SECRET INGREDIENT CHOCOLATE CAKE & GLAZE

A JIG ON A TUB & A TOAST TO ST. PAT

CORNED BEEF & CABBAGE

SOUR CREAM ROLLS

SHIRLEY'S OATMEAL LACE COOKIES

ST. PATRICK'S IRISH COFFEE

PAPPY AND THE LEPRECHAUN

Easter 1956

Jess Mays, my great-grandfather, was affectionately called Pappy by everyone. Pappy was a first generation Irish-American and the eldest son of Ruben Mays. Ruben had journeyed from Ireland to America at age three with his father.

Like his father before him, Ruben Mays instilled in Pappy a love of the Irish and for Ireland itself. I was Pappy's first great-grandchild, and when I was but a wee lass, he announced with great pride that I had been born with an "Irish soul."

Pappy's endearing family stories of Ireland and the leprechauns spun a magic thread though time and space from my heart to the Irish meadows-- and it has only grown stronger with time. Pappy had been right, my soul was as Irish as if I had been born on the Emerald Isle.

I never saw a leprechaun, but with Pappy I always found evidence of their existence. At Christmas he told me not to be fooled -- that it was leprechauns who made toys -- not elves. The proof was right there on the bottom of the foot of my hand-carved doll - a tiny shamrock. But, without a doubt, Pappy and the leprechaun's most convincing performance was Easter of 1956.

After my arrival on that long-ago Saturday afternoon, Pappy had taken me for a walk in the woods. He told me that I must never tell anyone what I was about to see.

Before me, stood a grand oak tree with a little door just above its roots. When I pulled open the door, there to my astonishment in the small space, was a tiny wooden bed and chair. In a serious tone, Pappy explained that he had followed the leprechaun through the woods to his home. But upon the realization that his home had been discovered, he had moved. "Perhaps," Pappy said, "the leprechaun has gone for good. We will just have to wait and see." "But what about my Easter eggs?" I cried. For, as with all other things, Pappy had taught me that leprechauns brought the Easter eggs.

On Easter morning, Pappy quietly awoke me with a "Lass, follow me." With zeal, Pappy said, "Faith and be durn!" For there on the edge of the woods, were tiny footprints leading down a path. My heart leaped, the leprechaun was still there! With a hush, we followed the footprints to a straw nest filled with the most beautiful Easter eggs I had ever seen.

One of Pappy's favorite sayings was that, "The Irish believe in impossible things just long enough to make them come true." I have yet to see a leprechaun, but from time to time my heart does see tiny footprints in the woods.

EASTER 1956 SUNDAY DINNER MENU

Succulent Baby Ribs

Onion Fried Potatoes

Irish Soda Bread

Marmalade Bread Pudding

"Pappy" Jess Mays - Easter 1956

Angie Thompson Holtzhouser - 1956

The Leprechaun

Ruben Mays - 1895

Succulent Baby-Back Ribs

Just the thought of these ribs makes my mouth water!

4   tablespoons oil
3   pounds baby-back pork ribs or beef short ribs
1   medium onion, chopped
4   tablespoons brown sugar
4   tablespoons Worcestershire sauce
1   cup tomato sauce
½   cup catsup
2   tablespoons vinegar

Preheat oven to 325 degrees.

1.   **Heat** oil in a large iron or other heavy ovenproof skillet, and brown ribs well.
2.   **Drain** off excess fat and add chopped onions.
3.   **Mix** remaining ingredients together and pour over ribs.
4.   **Cover** and bake at 325 degrees for 1 to 1½ hours, or until tender and meat pulls easily from the bone.

YIELD: 6 servings

Onion Fried Potatoes

A popular dinner dish in both the Southern United States and Ireland, these potatoes are often accompanied by a glass of buttermilk!

5	large potatoes
½	cup cooking oil
½	cup bacon drippings*
1	large onion, chopped
½	teaspoon salt
½	teaspoon garlic salt
½	teaspoon black pepper

1. **Peel** potatoes and slice ¼-inch thick.
2. **Heat** oil and bacon drippings in a large iron or heavy skillet over medium heat, and add potato slices.
3. **Turn** potatoes frequently with a spatula.
4. **After** 5 minutes, add salt, garlic salt, pepper and onions to potatoes.
5. **Cook,** turning frequently until potatoes are tender and browned around the edges.
6. **Lift** potatoes out with a slotted server and drain on paper towels.
7. **Serve** immediately.
   *If desired, vegetable oil can be subsituted, but the flavor will not be as rich.

YIELD: 6 servings

Ruben's Fancy Irish Soda Bread

No Irish or Irish-American household would be without soda bread -- for special occasions -- and for no occasion at all. Best eaten as soon as made, with a dollop of butter, Irish soda bread is as easy to make as biscuits. This was my great-great-grandfather Ruben's favorite bread.

3 cups self-rising flour
¼ teaspoon cream of tartar
1 tablespoon sugar
½ stick chilled margarine
½ cup currants or raisins, optional
1⅓ cups buttermilk

Preheat oven to 375 degrees.

1. **Combine** the self-rising flour, cream of tartar and sugar in a bowl.
2. **Cut** in the margarine with a pastry blender, or your fingers, until the mixture is mealy.
3. **Add** currants or raisins (if using) and the buttermilk; stir to blend well. Turn the dough out onto a floured board and knead briefly.
4. **Roll** dough into a flattened ball and place in an 8-inch iron skillet. Using a sharp knife, make a large X across the top of the dough.
5. **Place** the cover on the skillet and bake in preheated oven 25-30 minutes. Remove the cover and continue baking until golden brown. Remove from the oven, brush soda bread with melted butter and let stand in the skillet about 10 minutes before turning out onto a rack to cool.
6. **Serve** warm with plenty of butter.

YIELD: one 8-inch round loaf.

Irish Marmalade Bread Pudding

My great-grandmother's homemade orange marmalade was a first-cousin to Irish marmalade, with its tart slivers of orange peel and sweet jelly base. Traditional Irish marmalade is one of the joys of the Irish breakfast table. Here, it is used to flavor a simple bread pudding.

> 3½ cups sliced bread cubes
> 2   tablespoons melted butter
> 3   eggs, lightly beaten
> ⅓   cup brown sugar, plus 1 tablespoon for topping
> ½   cup Irish or other orange marmelade
>   pinch of salt
> 3   cups milk (skim or regular)

Preheat oven to 350 degrees.

1. **Place** the bread cubes in a mixing bowl.
2. **Combine** remaining ingredients (except 1 tablespoon of brown sugar for topping) and pour over the bread cubes. Stir to moisten. If bread is dry, let stand 15 minutes.
3. **Pour** pudding into a greased 2-quart souffle dish. Sprinkle with remaining tablespoon of brown sugar. Bake 45-50 minutes, or until brown and knife inserted in center of pudding comes out clean.

YIELD: 4 servings.

KNIGHT OF THE ROUND TABLE

Dwight Mays was born my cousin, but over the years he became the brother of my heart. I often thought that if Dwight had lived in the days of old, with his noble nature and handsome face, that he would have been one of King Arthur's Knights of the Round Table.

We spent many hours on the banks of the Mississippi River talking and eating Hummingbird Cake which was Dwight's favorite. This was a pastime that we carried into adulthood.

On a clear summer day in 1986 the unthinkable happened - we lost Dwight in a boating accident. Forever gone were the laughing blue eyes, and the fine young man that we had known.

Often, I still find myself on the banks of the Mississippi talking to Dwight; and I am very sure that on occassion I hear the clank of his armor as he takes his seat at the greatest Round Table of them all.

We love you, and we miss you.

The Mays family in 1960 - Chris, Patty Gail, Dwight & Herbert.

Hummingbird Cake

Dwight's favorite cake.

It is said that this cake is so good, even the elusive hummingbird can be lured to the ground by its sweet nectar crumbs.

3	**cups self-rising flour**
2	**cups sugar**
	dash of salt
1	**teaspoon cinnamon**
3	**eggs, beaten**
1	**cup corn oil**
1	**teaspoon pure vanilla extract**
1	**8-ounce can crushed pineapple (undrained)**
1	**cup small pecan pieces**
2	**cups chopped bananas (not mashed)**

Preheat oven to 350 degrees.

1. **Combine** first four ingredients in a large mixing bowl.
2. **Add** eggs and oil, stirring until all ingredients are moistened (do not beat).
3. **Stir** in vanilla extract, pineapple, pecans and bananas.
4. **Spoon** batter into three well-greased 9-inch cake pans.
5. **Bake** at 350 degrees for 30 minutes or until an inserted wooden pick comes out clean.
6. **Cool** on wire rack for 15 minutes.
7. **Remove** cake from pans and frost with Cream Cheese Frosting (p. 26).

YIELD: 12 servings

Cream Cheese Frosting

1   8-ounce package cream cheese, softened
2   sticks butter, softened
1   16-ounce box powdered sugar
½   teaspoon pure vanilla extract
½   cup pecan pieces

1. **Combine** first four ingredients, and beat at high speed until light and fluffy.
2. **Frost** cake.
3. **Sprinkle** pecan pieces on top.

YIELD: Enough frosting for a two or three 9-inch layer cake.

MAKING MUSIC ON SATURDAY NIGHT

You could buy everything from gas to a fresh-sliced bologna sandwich at my Granddaddy Thompson's country store. The old red drink box was filled with Orange Crush, Grape Nehi and Royal Crown Cola. Moon Pies were the size of the moon, and the candy counter whispered your name.

Of all the store's delights, the banana stalk was my favorite. Rather than purchasing bananas by the bunch, Granddaddy bought them by the stalk. Usually, the stalk was about four feet long and hung from a ceiling hook. You would choose the "just-right" banana and pluck that sucker right off the stalk. I can tell you that I ate a fair number of bananas during my childhood!

Thompson's Grocery was well-known in Hardin County, Tennessee, for Granddaddy's cheerful welcome made the store a favorite gathering place. There was always at least one good conversation coming from the social corner of the store, where two large benches nestled against the wall; but the lofty reputation for hand-clapping, foot-stomping music that was often performed on Saturday nights brought visitors from far and near -- some to listen-- others to perform.

On those carefree afternoons I was in a state of bliss, as I made a path from the excitement in the store where the men were setting up for the music-making, to Granny Thompson's kitchen where all the women had gathered to make "company-is-coming" desserts. Three that always graced the table were Secret Ingredient Chocolate Cake, Crazy Crust Pie and Drop Donuts. Sweet aromas filled the air, begging you to steal at least one donut!

Granddaddy played a mean fiddle and a wicked guitar, but the banjo was his forte. His banjo music caressed the good-time part of your spirit making you believe, at least for the moment, that you were good at singing and dancing.

You never knew who would show up. One Saturday night in the summer of 1963, when I was twelve years old, a stranger with a white Spanish guitar came to play. I don't know what enthralled me more, his dark good-looks or his soul-stirring music.

Most of the performers were family members-- with Granddaddy on the fiddle and banjo, Aunt Odessa and Uncle Wayne on guitars, cousin Harbet on the steel guitar, cousin Freddie on drums and piano; and the rest of us just joining "right-in-there" with the hand-clapping and foot-stomping! The old building vibrated with laughter and melody. Those were the sounds of memories being made.

Most of these grand and talented musicians now play for St. Peter in heaven's Crystal Square; and, forever, in a little corner of my heart.

Left to right: Granddaddy Thompson, Uncle Wayne,
Aunt Lou and Aunt Odessa.

Granddaddy and Granny Thompson
Richard Floyd and Alma Morris Thompson

Secret Ingredient Chocolate Cake

Orange juice gives this chocolate cake an interesting flavor. My Granny Thompson always used fresh orange juice.

1	cup corn oil
2	cups sugar
3	eggs
⅓	cup water
⅔	cup orange juice
3	cups self-rising flour
½	teaspoon pure vanilla extract
¾	cup chocolate syrup
¼	teaspoon baking soda

Preheat oven to 350 degrees.

1. **Cream** oil and sugar together.
2. **Add** eggs one at time, and beat until fluffy.
3. **Add** flour, alternately with water and orange juice.
4. **Blend** in vanilla extract.
5. **Pour** two-thirds of batter into a well-greased 10-inch bundt pan.
6. **Add** chocolate syrup and baking soda to remaining one-third of batter. Blend well.
7. **Pour** this mixture over the batter in pan.
8. **Bake** 35 minutes at 350 degrees. Reduce heat to 325 degrees and bake 25 minutes longer or until cake tests done.
9. **Cool** thoroughly on rack. Invert onto cake plate, and top with Orange Glaze (p. 32).

YIELD: 12 servings.

Orange Glaze

1¼ cups powdered sugar
1   tablespoon butter, softened
¼   cup orange juice
¼   teaspoon pure vanilla extract

1. **Mix** all ingredients until smooth. Add more juice if a thinner consistency is desired.
2. **Spread** or slowly pour over cake.

Aunt Lou's Crazy Crust Pie

Here's Aunt Lou's quick way to make a lip-smackin' cobbler!

1   **stick butter**
½   **cup sugar**
½   **cup brown sugar**
½   **teaspoon pure vanilla extract**
½   **teaspoon cinnamon**
1   **cup self-rising flour**
1   **cup evaporated milk**
4   **cups sweetened fruit**
         OR
2   **cans fruit pie filling**

Preheat oven to 350 degrees.

1. **Melt** ½ stick butter in a 9x13 baking dish.
2. **Cream** ½ stick butter, sugars and vanilla extract.
3. **Combine** cinnamon and flour.
4. **Add** to creamy mixture alternately with milk.
5. **Pour** over melted butter in baking dish.
6. **Top** with fruit - DO NOT stir.
7. **Bake** for 45 minutes.
8. **Serve** warm with ice cream or whipped cream.

YIELD: 6 servings

Drop Donuts

Hand-held goodies.

2   cups self-rising flour
¼   cup sugar
½   teaspoon cinnamon
¼   cup corn oil
¼   cup milk
 1   egg

2 cups vegetable oil, for frying
Cinnamon sugar or powdered sugar, for topping

1. **Mix** self-rising flour, sugar and cinnamon.
2. **Combine** corn oil, milk and egg.
3. **Add** wet ingredients to dry, stirring with fork until well-mixed.
4. **Pour** oil into skillet to depth of 2-inches. Heat to medium-high (360 degrees).
5. **Drop** batter by teaspoonfuls into hot oil, and fry until golden brown (2 to 3 minutes).
6. **Drain** on paper towels.
7. **Roll** donuts in mixture of cinnamon and sugar or sprinkle with powdered sugar.
8. **Serve** warm.

YIELD: 36 donuts.

A JIG ON A TUB & A TOAST TO ST. PAT

Pappy Mays turned the old tin wash tub upside-down, for its flat bottom gave me the perfect stage to perform the Irish jig at age three. Pappy whistled "A Toast to St. Patrick," and I kept time. Thus, St. Patrick's Day had officially begun in 1955.

Soon we would be eating corned beef and cabbage, as "Mike and Pat jokes" were told. My favorite one -- Mike says to Pat, "Can you see that fly walking on that wire way over there?" Pat takes a deep breath and says, "No, but I can hear him!" Everyone's favorite Irishmen, Mike and Pat, were full of shamrock shenanigans.

When Pappy crossed over the rainbow into clouds of green, my Mother carried on the Irish tradition. When I was about seven, she gave me a tiny gold leprechaun seated on a shamrock. I called him Ruben in honor of Pappy's father who had come from Ireland. Ruben is my lucky charm, and has been my companion for thirty-nine years.

We now have a large family gathering at my Mother and Daddy's on St. Patrick's Day for an Irish feast; to sing a song or two, "When Irish Eyes are Smiling;" and to give a toast-of-love, for all the sons and daughters of Erin before us and for all those to come.

ST. PATRICK'S DAY FARE

Corned Beef & Cabbage

Sour Cream Rolls

Shirley's Oatmeal Lace Cookies

Irish Coffee

Corned Beef & Cabbage

In Ireland, St. Patick's Day would not be complete without boiled bacon and cabbage. But, when Irish settlers, like my great-great grandparents came to America, bacon was too expensive to use as a main dish, so most families used corned beef instead. This dish offers the essence of the Emerald Isle in every bite.

1	**5-pound package ready-to-cook corned beef**
2	**large onions, sliced**
6	**medium potatoes, peeled and left whole**
6	**carrots, peeled and sliced lengthwise**
1	**large head cabbage, quartered and sliced**

1. **Remove** the corned beef from the package and rinse under cold water.
2. **Place** beef in a 4-6 quart pot and cover with cold water. Add the onions and bring to a boil. Reduce heat and simmer, partially covered, approximately 1 hour per pound of beef or until a fork can be inserted in the center of the meat.
3. **Add** the potatoes to the pot and continue cooking 15 minutes. Add the carrots and cook 5 minutes. Add the cabbage, and continue cooking 10-15 minutes, or until all the vegetables are done and the meat is fork-tender.
4. **Remove** the meat to a cutting board and slice thinly across the grain. Drain the vegetables.
5. **Arrange** the corned beef on a platter, surrounded by the vegetables. Moisten with a little of the cooking liquid. If desired, serve with mustard on the side.

YIELD: 8 servings.

Sour Cream Rolls

Light, melt-in-your-mouth goodness.

1   **cup sour cream**
1   **stick butter, melted**
1   **cup self-rising flour**

Preheat oven to 400 degrees.

1.   **Lightly** grease a 6-muffin size tin.
2.   **Mix** ingredients in medium bowl in order given.
3.   **Spoon** batter into greased muffin tin, filling cups halfway.
4.   **Bake** at 400 degrees for 20 minutes, or until lightly browned.

YIELD: Makes 6 rolls.

Shirley's Oatmeal Lace Cookies

Shirley Perry's twist on the original Irish oatmeal cookie is delicious. Oatmeal is a basic Irish staple that found new meaning in the hands of this Mississippi River woman, who is a dear friend.

2   **sticks margarine**
3   **cups oatmeal**

4   **tablespoons flour**
1½ **cups sugar**
    pinch of salt

2   **eggs slightly beaten**
2   **teaspoons pure vanilla extract**
1   **cup pecan nut pieces**

Preheat oven to 350 degrees.

1. **Melt** margarine and pour over oatmeal.
2. **Combine** flour, sugar and salt; add to oatmeal mixture.
3. **Add** eggs, vanilla and pecans.
4. **Drop** by teaspoonfuls onto aluminum foil.
5. **Bake** at 350 degrees for 10 minutes, or until edges show slightest sign of browning.
6. **Cool**, then PEEL cookies off the foil.

YIELD: 4 dozen cookies

St. Patrick's Irish Coffee

A cup of steaming Irish Coffee makes you feel special. And, it's a fitting finale to any St. Patrick's Day feast!

For each serving:

    2   **tablespoons Irish whiskey**
    1   **teaspoon brown sugar**
    ⅔   **cup strong coffee**
    3   **tablespoons heavy cream, lightly whipped**

1. **Fill** an Irish or regular coffee mug with hot tap water to warm.
2. **Pour** out water and add sugar and whiskey.
3. **Stir** well, while pouring in hot, strong coffee.
4. **Top** with heavy cream -- and sip the warm liquid through the cool layer of cream!

NOTE: It is important to use strong coffee so that the Irish whiskey complements it, rather than overpowers it.

YIELD: 1 serving

Rosie's
BAR & GRILLE

Presents

Appetizers
and
Beverages

BAR & GRILLE

ROSIE'S BAR & GRILLE, in New Madrid, Missouri, is the home of classic sandwiches, sensational salads and juicy prime rib cooked to perfection. The name "Rosie's" has been synonomus with good food for over 50 years.

In the early 1940's the idea for **ROSIE'S BAR & GRILLE** was born when the late Ms. Rosie Cowan opened the doors of Rosie's Restaurant. The location has changed several times over the years, but the commitment to excellence has stayed the same.

In 1963, Rosie's moved to its present location on Highway 61 North under the ownership of HAPCO, and evolved into **ROSIE'S BAR & GRILLE** -- where delicious meals are still the order of the day.

In June of 1997, HAPCO furthered its interest in fine dining opportunities, with the opening of a catering service in the "RIVERS" Building, which coincidentally is a former site of the original Rosie's Resturant. Aptly named "RIVERS", the building is located in New Madrid's historic downtown area, within walking distance of the mighty Mississippi River. The "RIVERS" Building is available for various functions and social events.

ROSIE'S BAR & GRILLE
Highway 61 North
New Madrid, MO 63869
573-748-7665

HAPCO
"Rivers" Building
537 Mott Street
New Madrid, MO 63869

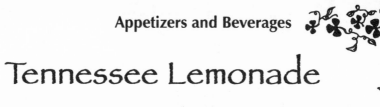

Tennessee Lemonade

Some folks add a touch of Jack Daniel's to this Southern favorite, but we like it plain.

1½ cups sugar
½ cup boiling water
1 cup fresh-squeezed lemon juice
5 cups cold water
6 lemon slices
   ice cubes
   fresh mint leaves

1. **Place** sugar and boiling water in a 2-quart pitcher and stir until sugar is dissolved.
2. **Add** lemon juice, cover and store in refrigerator until ready to use. Chill for at least 6 hours, but no longer than 24 hours.
3. **Add** cold water when ready to serve, and finish filling pitcher with lemon slices and ice cubes.
4. **Pour** over ice cubes in 12-ounce glasses. Use mint leaves for garnish, if desired.

YIELD: 6 servings

ANGIE AND THE HOT TODDY

Since I'm never going to live this one down, I'm going to be the one to tell it. I think that I shall be kinder to myself than anyone else will be.

After about three days of the worst chest cold that I have ever had, I was seeking relief anywhere I could find it. Being a teetotaller, a hot toddy cure did not occur to me, but it certainly did to a small gathering of my friends.

They told me that I was to mix brandy, two tablespoons of honey and the juice of a lemon to make a six-ounce toddy. What they assumed that I knew was that you added equal amounts of brandy and water to make the six ounces.

I called my husband and asked him to go get the brandy for me before he went to work at three o'clock that afternoon. He asked me if I was I sure I knew how to mix the toddy, and I assured him I did.

When I arrived home there it was on the kitchen counter - the brandy. Hurriedly, I squeezed the lemon juice into my cup, spooned in the honey and poured in the brandy. I added no water. The forty-five seconds in the microwave seemed liked an eternity. Finally, in my hands was the cure for what ailed me.

I turned the cup up and took a big gulp.   I was on fire-- I couldn't breathe-- and I couldn't see. When my sight and breathing returned, I realized that my chest felt better. So, I downed the rest of that awful hot toddy.

Strangely enough, two hours later, the second hot toddy I drank tasted better than the first one. The third one wasn't bad at all. I was feeling better all the time.

As I waited for my husband to return home at eleven o'clock that night, I prepared my fourth and last hot toddy, for I was out of brandy. That was OK -- I felt good-- really good!

When my husband returned home, I swung around the hall archway and said, "Hiiii! I feel so much better!" With great concern in his voice, he asked where the brandy bottle was. I told him that it was all gone. Over and over, he said that I couldn't have drunk it all, but I continued to assure him that I had.

Immediately, he attempted to make me drink coffee as he uttered something about alcohol poisoning and me being drunk. I thought he was being a stick-in-the-mud about me feeling better. After a great effort on his part, I drank a little coffee, and then he put me to bed.

When morning came my chest cold was better-- but my head felt like someone had used it for batting practice. I was in a state of motionlessness the rest of the day. Every time my husband looked at me he broke into laughter. This is his favorite story about me.

Angie's Hot Toddy

juice of one lemon
2 tablespoons honey
2 ounces brandy
2 ounces water

1. **Mix** all ingredients in small saucepan and heat until steaming.
2. **Ingredients** may also be mixed in a cup and heated in microwave.

YIELD: 1 serving

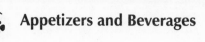

WHITE LIGHTIN' PARTY PUNCH

My Mother concocted this simple-to-make punch more than thirty-five years ago. The golden color is eye-catching, and it tastes like you are in the midst of a celebration.

One such celebration ensued on a spring afternoon in 1962, when my Mother and a close friend were hosting a bridal shower. It was an affair to remember. Everything was perfect, right down to Mother's revered "Golden Party Punch."

A couple of good-hearted husbands had helped set up tables and chairs-- and the punch bowl.

The ladies in all their finery, lovely spring hats and white gloves, were having one rip-roaring time. The usual so-so shower games suddenly were a riot. Everyone said that the punch was the best that Mother had ever made. By the time the bride-to-be was opening her gifts, the ladies found even a toaster and mixer to be hilarious.

It was about this time that they realized that the punch bowl was bone-dry. A dozen or so ladies had downed three gallons of punch, and certainly were all the merrier for it.

When the good-hearted husbands returned to take down the tables and chairs, they were more than amused to find that the ladies had drunk every drop of the punch. For, you see, one of these conscientious husbands was also the town prankster, and he had spiked the punch with white lightin'.

Those charming ladies never acknowledged that the punch had been spiked, but for years, that shower was recalled with a sparkle in their eyes and just a bit of laughter.

White Lightin' Party Punch

2   large bottles white grape juice
½   gallon fresh or frozen lemonade
½   gallon orange-pineapple juice
    (frozen or from the dairy section)
1   750ml bottle of rum or brandy (optional)

1. **Mix** all juices together the night before and refrigerate.
2. **Make** an ice ring by filling and freezing a ring mold with the punch mixture. This will not dilute your punch like a water ice ring.
3. **Pour** punch into bowl. If using the optional rum or brandy, stir it in. Add punch ice ring and garnish with fresh mint leaves and fruit slices, if desired.

YIELD: About 36 six-ounce servings

Café Brulôt Diabolique Royal N'Orleans Style

The **Royal N'Orleans Restaurant**, in Cape Girardeau, Missouri, uses gold-plated cups to enhance enjoyment of this fantastic libation!

2   sticks cinnamon
8   whole cloves
3   generous slices of lemon
3   generous slices of orange
1½ tablespoons sugar
3   ounces brandy
3   cups hot strong black coffee

1. **Combine** cinnamon sticks, cloves, lemon slices, orange slices and sugar with the brandy in a fireproof pan.
2. **Heat** in a chafing dish over an open flame, or using a stove burner, until the brandy is hot, but not boiling.
3. **Light** the brandy carefully with a match, and, while flaming, present it to your guests.
4. **Agitate** the flaming liquid in the pan using a ladle-- with   stirring and pouring motions-- for about two minutes, or until the flames subside. This will allow the mixture to marinate and become a spicy, potent concoction.
5. **Pour** the hot coffee into the brandy mixture.
6. **Ladle** café brulôt into cups, through tea strainer or slotted ladle to hold back seeds, peels and spices.

YIELD: 3 servings

Stuffed Mushrooms

*One of life's ultimate time-consuming joys is the slow pace of cruising down the Mississippi River aboard a **Memphis Queen Line Riverboat**. As the boat leaves the dock, one can start off a wonderful evening with every bite of these crab and shrimp stuffed mushroom appetizers.*

25	cleaned mushroom caps, medium to large
½	pound of butter
1	small onion, chopped fine
⅓	pound baby shrimp
2-3	cans crabmeat and liquid
	plain bread crumbs
½	teaspoon dried dill weed
½	teaspoon dried tarragon
2	teaspoons dried parsley
2	teaspoons dried basil leaves
½	teaspoon dried marjoram
½	teaspoon dried rosemary
	salt and pepper to taste
1	clove garlic, minced
	juice of ½ lemon

Preheat oven to 350 degrees.

1. **Wash** mushrooms and remove stems; scoop out some of the mushroom wall and bottom, being careful not to break. Reserve the stems and mushroom pieces.
2. **Melt** butter in a large saucepan. Sauté onions, chopped stems and mushroom pieces until onions are soft but not brown.
3. **Add** shrimp and crabmeat. Sauté, about 5 minutes.
4. **Add** enough bread crumbs to make mixture the consistency of dressing-- not wet, but not real dry.
5. **Add** dill, tarragon, parsley, basil leaves, marjoram, rosemary, salt, pepper, garlic and lemon juice. Sautè, for 5 minutes more.
6. **Stuff** mushrooms and bake in 350 degree oven for 15 minutes or until lightly browned.
   YIELD: 25 stuffed mushrooms

"Hello" Spinach Dip

*Not your ordinary spinach dip! A much requested item on the **Memphis Queen Line Riverboats**, this dip says "hello" with every bite. It's the perfect accompaniment to a beautiful Mississippi River sunset--on the Queen Line's famous dinner cruises.*

1   medium onion, chopped
2   tablespoons olive oil
1½ pounds fresh tomatoes, seeded and diced
     <u>or</u>
1½ pounds canned, Roma tomatoes, diced
     (drain juice before weighing tomatoes)
2   tablespoons jalapeño pepper
10 ounces frozen chopped spinach, thawed and squeezed dry
7   ounces Monterey Jack Cheese
8   ounces cream cheese, cut into ½-inch cubes, softened
1   cup half and half
2¼ ounces black olives, sliced
1   tablespoon red wine vinegar
     salt and pepper to taste

Preheat oven to 350 degrees

1. **Sauté**, onions in oil until softened. Add tomatoes and sauté, for 5 minutes more.
2. **Combine**, in a large bowl, the jalapeño peppers, spinach, cheese, cream cheese, half and half, olives, vinegar, salt and pepper. Add hot onion and tomato mixture. Mix well.
3. **Pour** into a 2-quart baking dish. Bake at 350 degrees for 35 minutes or until bubbly and lightly browned.
4. **Serve** with tortilla chips.

YIELD: 8 servings

LAMBERT'S CAFE
HOME OF THROWED ROLLS

Presents

Breads

LAMBERT'S "THROWED ROLL CAFE"

On March 13, 1942, Earl and Agnes Lambert, with 14 cents between them, borrowed $1500.00 and with 5 employees opened for business in downtown Sikeston, Missouri. **Lambert's** consisted of a 9-stool counter and 8 tables for a total seating capacity of 41 people.

Earl Lambert passed away in 1976, and his son Norman, and wife Patti, entered into the restaurant business as partners to Agnes Lambert. On a busy, crowded day, Norm was passing around extra rolls, when-- unable to reach a customer in the corner -- Norm threw the roll. The "throwed roll" was the beginning of a legend. In 1988, **Lambert's** moved to a new location with seating for 300, and the legend continues to grow.

Generous servings and "throwed rolls" have drawn customers from around the world. **Lambert's "Throwed Roll Cafe"** has been on all the National television networks, the Armed Forces Network, and German televion. And editorials have appeared in newspapers in all 50 states, and in Jane & Michael Stern's nationally syndicated column.

But, perhaps, Mr. Mo. and his regionally-read column, "Show Me Dining," said it best: "There may be better down-home country cooking than **Lambert's**, somewhere in Missouri, but I haven't found it. And, there can't possibly be a restaurant in the midwest that is more eccentric than this one. Lambert's is a Missouri Bootheel institution and is not to be missed. Give **Lambert's** "four hats!"

THREE LOCATIONS: 2515 East Malone
Sikeston, Missouri 63801
573-471-4261

Highway 65 Between	2981 S. McKenzie
Springfield & Branson, Missouri	Foley, Alabama
417-581-Roll (7655)	334-943-Roll (7655)

Ellie's Angel Biscuits

When my little granddaughter Ellie was born, she whispered "in my ear" that when she was living in "heaven's bud garden," the Angels would flake off tiny morsels of their biscuits for the "babies' daily bread."

This heavenly dough can be kept refrigerated for up to 5 days.

2   packages dry yeast
3   tablespoons lukewarm water
5   cups self-rising flour
½   teaspoon baking soda
¼   teaspoon salt
¼   cup sugar
¾   cup shortening
2   cups buttermilk
    melted butter to brush on biscuits

1. **Dissolve** yeast in lukewarm water.
2. **Sift** together dry ingredients; cut in shortening.
3. **Add** yeast and buttermilk to dry mixture. Mix well.
4. **Cover** and chill for at least six hours.
5. **Preheat** oven to 425 degrees.
6. **Take** out dough to be used; put remaining dough back in refrigerator.
7. **Turn** dough onto floured surface. Knead lightly and roll dough about ½-inch thick; cut with small biscuit cutter.
8. **Place** on a greased baking sheet and brush tops with melted butter. Bake 10 to 12 minutes or until lightly browned.

YIELD: 2½ to 3 dozen

Lambert's Throwed Rolls

On an extremely busy May day in 1976, Norm Lambert was attempting to pass out hot rolls to a standing-room-only lunch crowd, when a customer said, "Just throw the **** thing!" Norm did, starting the tradition of "throwed rolls" at **Lambert's Cafe** *in Sikeston, Missouri.*

Last year, Lambert's baked an average of 520 dozen rolls per day, for a grand total of 2,246,400 individual rolls. In the past 21 months, Lambert's has baked enough of their 5-inch in diameter rolls to reach 300 miles -- that's the distance between St. Louis, Missouri, and Memphis, Tennessee!

In 1996, **Lambert's** *customers buttered their "throwed rolls" with 1,927,800 little butter pats.*

5	eggs
3	ounces salt
2	pounds sugar
4	ounces yeast
14	ounces butter
4	quarts water
18	pounds all-purpose flour

1. **Mix** eggs, salt, sugar, yeast and butter. Add water and flour.
2. **Place** dough in roll pans and bake at 325 degrees for 15 minutes.

YIELD: 144 rolls

NOTE: Adapted recipe for **Lambert's Throwed Rolls** is on page **53**.

The following is an adapted recipe for Lambert's Throwed Rolls.

2   packages active dry yeast
½   cup warm water, 105-115 degrees
½   cup butter
2½ teaspoons salt
¼   cup sugar
2   cups hot water
2   eggs
4½ cups sifted all-purpose flour, or enough to make a soft
     dough

1. **Mix** yeast and warm water and let stand 5 minutes.
2. **Combine** butter, salt and sugar in a separate bowl. Pour hot water over butter mixture until sugar is dissolved. When luke-warm, add yeast; beat in egg.
3. **Stir** in flour and beat until blended.
4. **Put** dough in a large, greased bowl, cover with clean cloth or plastic wrap and let rise until doubled in bulk, about one hour. Punch dough down.
5. **Grease** a large muffin tin. Shape the rolls to fill cups in muffin tin to one-third full.
6. **Let** rise until double in bulk, about 40 minutes. While rolls are rising, preheat oven to 375 degrees. Bake rolls for 15 minutes or until golden brown. Serve hot.

YIELD: 36 rolls

Dixieland Shortcake

These fluffy delights, crowned with fresh fruit and whipped cream, are a delectable finale to any meal.

4   tablespoons vegetable shortening
4   cups self-rising flour
2   egg whites
1½ cups milk
      fresh fruit, cut up and sweetened, if necessary
      whipped cream

Preheat oven to 450 degrees.

1.   **Cut** shortening into flour until mealy.
2.   **Beat** egg whites until stiff, fold into milk; gradually add to flour mixture, mixing with a fork until soft ball forms.
3.   **Roll** dough ½-inch thick on lightly floured surface.
4.   **Cut** with 3-inch biscuit cutter; place on ungreased baking sheet.
5.   **Prick** with fork before baking in 450 degree oven for 10 minutes, or until lightly browned.
6.   **Split** shortcakes and layer with fresh fruit and whipped cream.

YIELD: 12 shortcakes

Almond Biscotti

These simple but delicious biscotti are a favorite of shoppers at the **Heavenly Brew Gourmet Coffee Shop** *in River Birch Mall, Sikeston, Missouri.*

5	cups Gold Medal or other variety muffin mix
1	cup all-purpose flour
3	large eggs
2	teaspoon pure almond extract
¾	teaspoon baking soda
1½	teaspoons vanilla extract
½	cup whole almonds

Preheat oven to 325 degrees

1. **Place** all ingredients in mixer bowl. Mix using a dough hook on low speed until well blended, 2 to 3 minutes.
2. **Divide** dough in half.
3. **Form** each half into 12 x 2-inch strip on parchment lined baking pan. Bake at 350 degrees for 25 minutes or until lightly browned.
4. **Cool** until baked strips can be handled; cut cross-wise into ¾-inch thick slices and place back on baking pan.
5. **Bake** slices at 300 degrees for 6 to 9 minutes on each side or until lightly browned.
6. **Transfer** to rack to cool. Store at room temperature in tightly covered container.

YIELD: About 2 dozen

Heirloom Vinegar Rolls

These "ole south" rolls are too good not to share! They were popular in the area where I grew up-- in the "Heart of Dixie"-- along the Tennessee/Alabama border.

¾ cup vinegar
1½ cups water
1   cup sugar
2   teaspoons cinnamon
2   cups self-rising flour
6   tablespoons vegetable shortening
¾ cup milk

¼ cup sugar
2   teaspoons cinnamon
4   tablespoons butter

Preheat oven to 375 degrees.

1. **Combine** vinegar, water, 1 cup sugar and 2 teaspoons cinnamon, stirring over low heat until sugar dissolves. Cook over medium heat for 20 minutes or until sugar crystals form around edge of mixture.
2. **Sift** flour into large bowl; cut in shortening until mealy. Stir in milk with fork until a soft dough forms.
3. **Roll** out dough into rectangle about ¼-inch thick.
4. **Combine** ¼ cup sugar with 2 teaspoons cinnamon and sprinkle over surface of rectangle. Dot with 2 tablespoons of the butter.
5. **Roll** up, starting at longer side. Cut crosswise into slices about 1¼ inches thick.
6. **Place** slices in a 9 x 13-inch baking dish. Dot with remaining 2 tablespoons of butter. Pour hot vinegar mixture over all.
7. **Bake** for 30 to 40 minutes or until golden brown. Serve hot, with heavy cream.

YIELD: 12 rolls

Mother's Praiseworthy Cornbread

My mother makes the world's best cornbread in her trusty old iron skillet greased with real bacon drippings. The outside of her cornbread is brown and crisp, and the inside so tender that it all but falls apart as you butter it.

1   **cup self-rising cornmeal mix**
1   **cup self-rising flour**
1   **egg**
¼   **cup vegetable oil or bacon drippings**
1¼ **cups milk**

¼   **cup vegetable oil or bacon drippings for skillet**

Preheat oven to 450 degrees.

1.   **Stir** together cornmeal and flour.
2.   **Add** egg, oil and milk, mixing well.
3.   **Heat** ¼ cup vegetable oil or bacon drippings in 10-inch iron skillet, over medium high heat, until very hot but not smoking.
4.   **Pour** batter into skillet. (If you do not have an iron skillet, use a 9 x 9 inch baking pan.)
5.   **Bake** about 20 minutes or until golden brown.

YIELD: 8 servings

Flavored Cornbread Muffins

*When it was decided that **DIAMONDS** Restaurant, at **Casino Aztar** in Caruthersville, Missouri, must have a great bread program, Chef Toni and all her helpers put their heads together and came up with some interesting flavors for your basic cornbread muffins. Barbara Hollywood created the basic recipe.*

Preheat oven to 350 degrees.

2   **cups self-rising cornmeal**
1   **cup self-rising flour**
2   **cups buttermilk**
3   **eggs**
½   **cup vegetable oil**

1.   **Mix**, all ingredients in order given, to the consistency of cake batter.
2.   **Fill** lightly-greased muffin pans two-thirds full and bake 10-12 minutes at 350 degrees.

YIELD: 24 muffins

FLAVORS - ALL TO TASTE

* Sugar or honey
* Jalapeños, chopped
* Creamed corn (very moist)
* Chicken bouillon powder and fresh mushrooms
* Fresh herbs - rosemary, thyme and basil

Diamonds' Apple Tomato Chutney

*Patrons of **DIAMONDS** Resturant at **Casino Aztar** find this zesty chutney to be the perfect accompaniment to their Flavored Cornbread.*

6   large ripe tomatoes, peeled and chopped
7   large apples, peeled and chopped
½   pound light brown sugar
2   tablespoon salt
4   tablespoons mustard seed
½   cup minced onion
1½ teaspoons tumeric
1   tablespoon ground ginger
1   tablespoon ground mustard
¼   cup red pepper, chopped
½   cup raisins, chopped
1½ pints cider vinegar

1. **Mix** all ingredients in a large pot and bring to a boil over medium heat. Lower temperature and simmer until liquid is absorbed.
2. **Cool** chutney. Put through food processor for a creamy texture.
3. **Store** in refrigerator.

YIELD: 3 pints

Sugar-Free Apple Nut Muffins

*This old recipe with a new twist is one of **Heavenly Brew Gourmet Coffee Shop's** best sellers. Located in the River Birch Mall, in Sikeston, Missouri -- just a hop, skip, 'n a jump -- from the Mississippi River-- Heavenly Brew's muffins are as popular with antique connoisseurs as they are with bargain shoppers.*

2	cups all-purpose flour
1	teaspoon baking soda
¼	teaspoon salt
¼	teaspoon ground ginger
¼	teaspoon nutmeg
¼	teaspoon allspice
2	tablespoons oat bran
2	large eggs
1	cup + 2 tablespoons frozen apple juice concentrate, thawed
⅔	cup buttermilk
2	small Granny Smith apples, chopped
1	cup walnut or pecan pieces

Preheat oven to 350 degrees -- Grease muffin pan

1. **Combine** all dry ingredients -- flour, baking soda, salt, ginger, nutmeg, allspice and oat bran-- in a large bowl.
2. **Combine** all wet ingredients -- eggs, apple juice and buttermilk --in a small bowl
3. **Pour** wet ingredients slowly into dry ingredients, blending well.
4. **Fold** in apples, then nuts. Spoon batter into muffin cups, to about ½ full.
5. **Bake** for 25 minutes or until golden brown.

YIELD: 12 muffins

Presents

Soups and Salads

CASINO AZTAR'S beautiful "City of Caruthersville" Riverboat Casino, with an 800 passenger capacity, arrived in Caruthersville, Missouri to a cheering crowds on April 1, 1995. Caruthersville is located on I-55, about 90 miles north of Memphis, Tennessee, and has one of the most scenic views of the mighty Mississippi River.

Later in 1995, **CASINO AZTAR'S** magnificent new pavilion opened — featuring **DIAMONDS** Restaurant; Sidelines Sports Bar; Dealers Choice Snack Bar and Memories Gift Shop. Fine dining, entertainment, shopping, sweepstakes and jackpots have all been a part of the exciting and fun experience of **CASINO AZTAR**. But that was not enough for Aztar Corporation.

In 1997 **CASINO AZTAR'S** Riverview Park opened with an Expo Center that is home to many events, including arts and crafts festivals; U.S.W.A. Wrestling, and country recording artist. The new center also contains a superior Rodeo Arena, where the Annual Casino Aztar July 4th Weekend Rodeo is held, horse shows and truck pulls. Outdoors, there is a scenic picnic area overlooking Ol' Man River".

CASINO AZTAR is committed to the Missouri Bootheel and surrounding area with major investments, real estate expansion and community involvement. **CASINO AZTAR** crewmembers are well known for their volunteer work, their friendliness and helpfulness. That's why "Aztar" has the honored status of being known as the **"COMMUNITY FRIENDLY"** Casino.

CASINO AZTAR
An Aztar Corporation Casino
* 777 E. 3rd Street * Caruthersville, MO 63830
573-333-6000   FAX: 573-333-1177

Red Snapper In Ginger Court Bouillon

*This recipe is compliments of John Wyman, Chef at the **Royal N' Orleans Restaurant**, in Cape Girardeau, Missouri.*

4   **8-ounce red snapper fillets**
2   **quarts light fish stock, or bouillon**
2   **tablespoons butter**
⅔   **cup dry white wine**
⅛   **cup white wine vinegar (same as 2 tablespoons)**
1   **cup onion, sliced**
½   **cup carrots, julienned**
½   **cup leeks, chopped**
½   **cup celery, chopped**
½   **cup zucchini, seeded and chopped**
¼   **cup red bell peppers, chopped**
1   **tablespoon cracked black peppercorns**
1   **garlic clove**
1   **bay leaf**
    dash cayenne pepper
    salt to taste
    fresh grated ginger to taste
    juice of ½ lemon

1.   **Boil** all ingredients, except the snapper, in a deep sauté, pan for 15 minutes.
2.   **Let** the mixture rest for 20 minutes, skimming if necessary.
3.   **Add** red snapper and bring liquid to a simmer. (Fillets should be submerged entirely.)
4.   **Cook** snapper for about 10 minutes or until done.
5.   **Remove** snapper to 4 shallow bowls. Bring liquid back to boil and reduce volume by ⅓.
6.   **Remove** garlic and bay leaf. Ladle finished bouillon and vegetables over snapper. Serve immediately.

YIELD: 4 servings

White Chili

*This is one of **The Blue Owl Restaurant and Bakery's** most popular soups. It blends white beans -- a staple of the southern Mississippi River region -- with the spicy flavors of the southwest.*

4   whole chicken breasts
1   tablespoon olive oil
2   medium onions, chopped
4   garlic cloves, minced
2   4-ounce cans chopped mild green chilies
2   teaspoons ground cumin
1½ teaspoons dried oregano, crumbled
¼   teaspoon cayenne pepper, optional
3   16-ounce cans Great Northern white beans
6   cups chicken stock or canned broth
3   cups grated Monterey Jack cheese
    salt and pepper to taste
    sour cream, optional

1. **Place** chicken breasts in large, heavy saucepan. Add cold water to cover and bring to simmer. Cook until just tender, about 15 minutes. Drain and cool. Remove skin. Cut chicken into cubes.
2. **Heat** oil in same pan over medium-high heat. Add onions and sauté, until translucent, about 10 minutes. Stir in garlic, then chilies, cumin, oregano and cayenne. Sauté, 2 minutes.
3. **Add** undrained beans and stock, and bring to a boil. Reduce heat and add chicken and cheese to chili. Stir until cheese melts.
4. **Season** to taste with salt and pepper. Ladle chili into bowls. Garnish with sour cream, if desired.

YIELD: 8 servings

Second-Helping Potato Soup

This rich soul-warming soup is a family favorite.

2   sticks butter
1   large onion, chopped
1   teaspoon salt
1   teaspoon garlic salt
½   teaspoon pepper
5   large baking potatoes
¼   cup fresh or dried celery leaves, chopped
½   cup heavy cream
½   cup milk
5   slices of American cheese

1.   **Melt** butter in a 4-quart saucepan; add onions, salt, garlic salt and pepper. Cook over medium heat until onions are clear and butter is a golden color. Remove from heat.
2.   **Peel** potatoes and cut 4 into medium size pieces and 1 into small thin pieces. Add to butter mixture. Add celery leaves.
3.   **Add** just enough water to cover top of potatoes. Simmer until potatoes are tender, stirring occasionally.
4.   **Add** cream and milk.
5.   **Add** cheese, stirring gently until melted.
6.   **Add** additional salt and pepper to taste, if needed.
7.   **Remove** from heat and let soup set for about 15 minutes to slightly thicken.

YIELD: 4 to 6 servings.

Beef Stew With Guinness

*Two staples of Irish life - beef and Guinness, the stout, dark ale --
come together in this richly-flavored stew. If you don't have
Guinness, any dark beer or ale can be used. This "one-pot" dish can
be made ahead of time, and an overnight stay in the fridge doesn't
hurt the flavor one bit ... it may even improve it! Pappy Mays could
remember his mother cooking this stew in a hanging pot in their
fireplace.*

2   **pounds beef stew meat, cut into 1½-inch cubes**
1   **cup flour, seasoned with salt, pepper and paprika**
2   **tablespoons butter**
2   **tablespoons oil**
1   **onion, diced**
1   **12-ounce bottle Guinness (dark ale)**
2   **cups water**
2   **tablespoons brown sugar**
1   **bay leaf**
     salt to taste
¼   **teaspoon freshly ground black pepper**
½   **pound carrots, peeled and cut into 1-inch chunks**
3   **stalks celery, cut into 1-inch slices**
3   **large potatoes, peeled and cut into cubes**
     chopped parsley for garnish

1. **Shake** the beef cubes in seasoned flour, shaking off the excess. Save leftover seasoned flour for thickening the stew later.
2. **Heat** the butter and oil in a large heavy pot and when the foam subsides, brown the beef, a few cubes at a time, removing them to a plate as they brown.
3. **Add** the onions to the pot and cook over medium heat until they soften and are beginning to brown, about 5 minutes.

4. **Replace** the beef in the pot, along with the Guinness, water, brown sugar, bay leaf, salt and pepper. Bring to a boil, reduce heat, cover and simmer about 1 hour, or until the beef is almost tender.
5. **Add** the carrots, celery and potatoes to the pot and continue cooking about 30 minutes, or until the meat is fully tender and the vegetables are done.
6. **Thicken** the stew a little more, if desired, by blending 2 tablespoons of the leftover seasoned flour with ⅓ cup of cold water and adding it to the hot stew. Cook a minute or two, stirring, until thickened.
7. **Serve** hot, in bowls, topped with chopped parsley.

    YIELD: 6 servings

Chef Toni's Turkey Reuben

*Chef Toni, the pride of **DIAMONDS** Restaurant at **Casino Aztar**, in Caruthersville, Missouri, introduced this delightful twist of a traditional Reuben, with lean meat and cole slaw, to Southeast Missouri.*

3   ounces smoked turkey
2   slices Swiss cheese
     creamy cole slaw (your favorite recipe)
2   slices rye bread

1.   **Butter** bread and grill.
2.   **Place** cheese on each slice of bread.
3.   **Grill** turkey, lightly, and place on bread. Top with cole slaw.
4.   **Place** bread together - grill until warmed and cheese melts.
5.   **Serve** with fresh fruit.

YIELD: 1 sandwich

Cole Slaw ~ Lambert's Style

*In a year's time, customers at **Lambert's Cafe**, in Sikeston, Missouri will eat 13,107 gallons of cole slaw, dressed with 2,091 gallons of mayonnaise. Think of the number of man hours required to shred the cabbage used in their slaw!*

5	pounds cabbage, shredded
5	carrots, grated
1	small head red cabbage, shredded
¼	cup sugar
½	gallon mayonnaise dressing

1. **Combine** all ingredients.
2. **Chill** until ready to serve.

YIELD: 40 servings

*The following is an adapted recipe for **Lambert's** cole slaw that is quick and good.*

1	package cole slaw mix
1	cup shredded red cabbage
1	tablespoon sugar
¼	cup cider vinegar
1	cup mayonnaise
	salt and pepper to taste

1. **Combine** all ingredients in a large bowl .
2. **Refrigerate** until ready to serve.

YIELD: 8 servings

Poppy Seed Dressing

This dressing, a specialty of the house at **Rosie's Bar & Grille** *in New Madrid, Missouri, turns a simple salad into a superb salad!*

¾ **cup sugar**
⅓ **cup white vinegar**
1½ **tablespoons onion juice**
¼ **teaspoon garlic juice**
1 **teaspoon dry mustard**
½ **teaspoon salt**
1 **cup vegetable oil**
1½ **tablespoons poppy seeds**

1. **Combine** the first 6 ingredients.
2. **Beat** in oil in slow, steady stream. Blend 1 minute or until thickened.
3. **Stir** in poppy seeds.

   YIELD: about 2½ cups

Larry DeWitt's Cilantro Salad

DeWitt, a horticulturist, landscape designer, and owner of the **River Birch Mall** *in Sikeston, Missouri, still finds time to pursue his favorite hobby -- cooking. Larry says that this salad is easy to mix and fun to eat.*

1	**bunch fresh cilantro**
1	**medium onion, diced**
½	**cup (or to taste) jalapeño pepper, seeds removed and diced***
2	**medium tomatoes, seeded and diced**
1	**teaspoon salt**
¼	**cup pure olive oil**

1. **Wash** cilantro thoroughly in cold water, making sure any sand is rinsed away; remove any tough stems.
2. **Chop** cilantro leaves and tender stems finely in a large bowl.
3. **Add** onion, jalapeño pepper, tomatoes, salt and olive oil. Toss until coated with olive oil.

   YIELD: 4 servings

   ***NOTE:** After preparation of jalapeño peppers, wash hands with soap and cold water.

Tonya's Spicy Chicken Salad

My Aunt Tonya's Spicy Chicken Salad recipe always makes me think of the afternoon that she was on the run-away riding lawn mower. "Spicy" and "colorful" were her shouts as she knocked down the gutters and the clothes line, and then on-- to mow a most creative pattern into her lawn and flower beds. That was an interesting sight to behold, and this chicken salad is just as interesting and colorful!

1	cup mayonnaise or light salad dressing
2	tablespoons honey
1	jalapeño pepper, seeded and chopped
½	teaspoon hot pepper sauce
½	teaspoon Worcestershire sauce
¼	teaspoon cayenne pepper
1	12-ounce package frozen breaded chicken breasts, cooked and sliced
2	cups lettuce, shredded
½	cup fresh tomatoes, diced
½	cup fresh mushrooms, sliced
¼	cup green pepper, chopped
¼	cup celery, chopped
¼	cup green onions, chopped

1. **Mix** mayonnaise or light salad dressing, honey, jalapeño pepper, hot pepper sauce, Worcestershire sauce and cayenne pepper.
2. **Place** chicken slices on lettuce.
3. **Top** with tomatoes, mushrooms, green pepper, celery and green onions. Lightly toss.
4. **Drizzle** with dressing.

YIELD: 4 servings

Lemon Pepper Dressing

*This dressing is a big hit at **Rosie's Bar & Grille** in New Madrid, Missouri, because it adds a tasty note to any salad.*

1	cup vegetable oil
¼	cup fresh lemon juice
¼	cup red wine vinegar
2	tablespoons brown mustard
4	cloves garlic, minced
1	teaspoon salt
1	teaspoon pepper
2	tablespoons green onions, sliced
½	cup green pepper, chopped

1. **Mix** first seven ingredients. Let stand for 30 minutes.
2. **Stir** in green onions and chopped peppers.
3. **Drizzle** over salad of your choice.

   YIELD: about 2½ cups

Corned Beef Pasta Salad

This is one of my family's favorite recipes!

6   hard-boiled eggs, chopped
12 ounces corned beef*, cut into pieces
4   cups cooked shell macaroni
½   cup red onion, chopped
½   cup green pepper, diced
½   cup celery, diced
     cherry tomatoes, if desired
     mayonnaise

1.   **Mix** all ingredients with amount of mayonnaise desired.
2.   **Salt** and pepper to taste.
3.   **Chill** well before serving.

YIELD: 4 servings

*NOTE: Ham or turkey may be used.

**Gourmet Shop and Cooking School
Memphis, Tennessee**

Presents

Vegetables
and
Side Dishes

FORTY CARROTS

Charismatic Phyllis Cline, who was once a fur buyer, decided more than ten years ago to turn her love of food and cooking into her life's work, and hence was born - **FORTY CARROTS** - noted for its fine gift selections and excellent gourmet items. **FORTY CARROTS** also features quality cooking classes where learning is fun, and nothing could be finer than catering by **FORTY CARROTS**, one of Memphis, Tennessee's finest.

One of Phyllis's favorite recipes is Pickled Carrots, served as a part of a large pickle and olive assortment.

Pickled Carrots

1½ cups cider vinegar
1½ cups water
1   cup sugar
2   tablespoons dill seeds
1   bay leaf
6   peppercorns
3   cloves garlic, sliced
2   pounds baby carrots

1. **Combine** vinegar, water and sugar in a large saucepan, and bring mixture to a boil, stirring until sugar dissolves.
2. **Add** dill seeds, bay leaf, peppercorns and garlic. Bring mixture to a boil over medium heat. Cover, reduce heat, and simmer 6 to 8 minutes. Remove mixture from heat.
3. **Pack** baby carrots into jars. Pour enough of liquid in jars to cover carrots. Cap and let jars cool, then refrigerate until ready to serve.

YIELD: 14 to 16 appetizer servings

FORTY CARROTS
Audubon Place
4690 Spottswood Ave.
Memphis, Tennessee 38117
901-683-5187

Creamy Corn Pudding

Here's down-home eatin' at its best! Make this when corn is at its summertime peak of perfection.

4	tablespoons butter
1	medium onion, chopped
¼	cup flour
¼	teaspoon pepper
1	teaspoon salt
½	teaspoon paprika
4	cups fresh or frozen corn kernels
2	eggs, beaten
1	cup milk
½	cup evaporated milk

Preheat oven to 350 degrees.

1. **Melt** butter in a small skillet and sauté, onions until softened. Remove from heat to cool.
2. **Combine** flour, pepper, salt and paprika in a large bowl.
3. **Fold** corn into flour mixture.
4. **Add** the beaten eggs and butter with sautéed onions.
5. **Add** both milks, mixing well.
6. **Pour** into a buttered 2-quart casserole dish.
7. **Bake**, uncovered, at 350 degrees for 30 to 40 minutes or until center is set.

YIELD: 6 servings

Glazed Lemon Carrots

Forty Carrots in Memphis, Tennessee, shares this tasty carrot recipe. It goes great with grilled chicken or pork for a light summer meal.

1   pound carrots, scraped and cut into ovals (or use packaged baby carrots)
½   teaspoon salt
4   tablespoons butter
½   teaspoon paprika
1   teaspoon minced parsley
1   tablespoon sugar
     zest of ½ lemon
     juice of ½ lemon

1.   **Simmer** carrots covered with water and salt in saucepan, until tender, about 10 minutes.
2.   **Drain**; add remaining ingredients to carrots in saucepan.
3.   **Sauté**, mixture for 10 minutes, stirring and shaking carrots to insure that each one is coated well with lemon mixture. Spoon into serving dish.

YIELD: 4 servings

"Just-Plain-Good" Hash-Brown Casserole

This old family favorite is especially good with smoked or baked ham.

8	cups frozen hash brown potatoes
1	cup chopped onions
½	cup melted butter
1	teaspoon salt
1	teaspoon garlic salt
1	teaspoon black pepper
2	cups grated cheddar cheese
1	5-ounce can evaporated milk
½	cup whole milk

Preheat oven to 350 degrees.

1. **Grease** a 9 x 13-inch or 11 x 15-inch pan.
2. **Layer** ingredients in order given: <u>1st Layer</u>: 4 cups hash browns, ½ cup onion, ¼ cup butter, ½ teaspoon each salt, garlic salt & pepper, and 1 cup cheddar cheese. <u>2nd Layer</u>: 4 cups hash browns, ½ cup onion, evaporated and whole milk; ½ teaspoon each salt, garlic salt and pepper; 1 cup cheddar cheese and ¼ cup butter.
3. **Bake** at 350 degrees for 45 minutes, or until golden brown.

YIELD: 8 servings

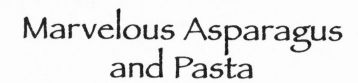

Marvelous Asparagus and Pasta

Even asparagus-haters will eat this delicious and easy dish -- a favorite in Southeast, Missouri, where asparagus is a big crop in almost every home garden.

3	cups spiral pasta
½	teaspoon salt
4	tablespoons olive oil
2	green onions, white part only
4	cloves garlic, minced
4	cups asparagus tips, cut into 1-inch pieces
1	tomato, peeled and cut into wedges
2	tablespoons dry white wine
½	teaspoon salt
½	teaspoon black pepper
¼	teaspoon paprika
¼	cup tomato, peeled and chopped

1. **Cook** the pasta in boiling water with ½ teaspoon salt until al dente (chewy), about 15 minutes.
2. **Heat** olive oil in a large skillet. Add green onions and garlic and cook, stirring occasionally, about 2 minutes over medium heat, taking care not to burn the garlic.
3. **Add** asparagus tips and tomato wedges. Sprinkle with salt, black pepper and paprika. Cook 5 minutes. Add wine, stirring well.
4. **Drain** cooked pasta and add to asparagus mixture. Stir gently over low heat until blended and hot.
5. **Arrange** on serving platter. Scatter chopped tomato over the top.

YIELD: 6 servings as side dish

Norm's White Beans

*In 1996, 40,800 pounds of white beans were served at **Lambert's Cafe**, in Sikeston, Missouri. The late Norm Lambert's secret ingredient in these white beans, as in all of Lambert's recipes, was the heart-felt hospitality he showed to each customer. Norm's great family is still on hand to add that same ingredient.*

2½ gallons of white beans
4   gallons of water
1   cup salt
2   whole onions
1   whole ham
1⅓ cups of hickory-flavored liquid smoke
½   cup black pepper

1. **Combine** all ingredients in very large pot.
2. **Cook** over low heat for 4 hours or until done.

YIELD: 75 servings

*The following is an adapted recipe for **Norm's White Beans**.*

1   pound white beans
8   cups water, more if needed during cooking
1   teaspoon salt
1   teaspoon black pepper
1   tablespoon hickory-flavored liquid smoke
2   tablespoons onion, chopped
½   pound ham, cubed or shredded

1. **Combine** all ingredients in 4-6 quart cooker. Simmer over low heat, stirring occasionally, for 2 hours or until done.
2. **Serve** with corn bread or rolls.

YIELD: 6-8 servings

Sweet Potato Crisp

*This is a house specialty at **The Blue Owl Restaurant and Bakery** in Kimmswick, Missouri. The cranberries add a touch of color and dash of flavor to this traditional dish. Great as a side-dish or dessert.*

1	8-ounce package cream cheese, softened
1	40-ounce can cut sweet potatoes, drained
¼	cup packed brown sugar
¼	teaspoon ground cinnamon
1	cup apples, chopped
⅔	cup cranberries
½	cup all-purpose flour
½	cup old-fashioned or quick oats, uncooked
½	cup packed brown sugar
⅓	cup margarine
¼	cup chopped pecans

Preheat oven to 350 degrees

1. **Beat** cream cheese, sweet potatoes, ¼ cup brown sugar and cinnamon in large mixing bowl at medium speed until well-blended.
2. **Spoon** into 1½-quart casserole or 10 x 6-inch baking dish; top with apples and cranberries.
3. **Stir** together flour, oats and ½ cup brown sugar in medium bowl; cut in margarine until mixture resembles coarse crumbs. Stir in pecans. Sprinkle over fruit.
4. **Bake** at 350 degrees for 35 to 40 minutes or until thoroughly heated.

   YIELD: 8 servings

Tootie's Ya'll Come Potato Salad

My mother-in-law is famous for her potato salad. It's simple, yet so good!

5	medium potatoes, unpeeled
4	eggs, boiled and chopped
1	small onion, chopped
1	small jar pimentos, drained and chopped
1	cup mayonnaise
1	teaspoon salt
½	teaspoon black pepper
	paprika for garnish

1. **Cook** unpeeled potatoes in water in large saucepan 30 minutes, or until tender. Drain and cool.
2. **Peel** and cut-up potatoes. Chop-up eggs.
3. **Combine** potatoes, eggs, onion, pimentos, mayonnaise, salt and pepper. Lightly mix until potatoes are evenly coated.
4. **Garnish** with paprika.
5. **Chill** at least 1 hour.

YIELD: 6 servings

Notes

The Royal N'Orleans

Presents

Entrées

THE ROYAL N'ORLEANS

THE ROYAL N'ORLEANS maintains a 40-year reputation in Cape Girardeau, Missouri, where it is known as one of the finest restaurants in the area. The original building was built in 1865 by the Turner Society. Shortly thereafter, a group of Masons purchased the building and turned it into The Opera House. The stage was located on the second floor while shops were on the first. Over the next one-hundred-and-twenty-years, the actual building would house many different businesses on the first floor, including the restaurant known as **THE ROYAL N'ORLEANS**.

In 1990, a fire almost ended the existence of this historic building. But, due to the efforts of Dennis Stockard, an area businessman and owner of **THE ROYAL N'ORLEANS** at the time, the building was saved and restored to its present grandeur. Jerri & John Wyman purchased the existing business and building in October of 1995.

THE ROYAL N'ORLEANS was started in 1954 by Mr. and Mrs. Dick Barnhouse. Their desire to create a creole style restaurant worthy of the Vieux Carré, has resulted in a 40-year tradition for Cape Girardeau where people from all over come to celebrate births, weddings, anniversaries, proms, graduations and other special events..

THE ROYAL N'ORLEANS, also known as "The Original Creole Steakhouse," is acclaimed for its outstanding steaks and chateaubriand for two. The menu also boasts fine seafood and pastas, lamb and chicken, and the chef's nightly specials -- prepared each day using fresh seasonal ingredients and herbs from THE ROYAL N'ORLEANS' own herb garden. **THE ROYAL N'ORLEANS'** "Oysters Casino" are a must for seafood lovers, and the restaurant's "King-Size Cocktails" are renowned.

THE ROYAL N'ORLEANS
300 Broadway
Cape Girardeau, Missouri 63701
573-335-8191
Visit our website: Cape dining.com

Christine's "Poppy-Kosh" Chicken

19th century America was a melting pot of people and food. My Aunt Chris' chicken recipe, which evolved through several generations, grew out of "Irish stew meeting Hungarian goulash." Then, rural Southern Irish accents turned "paprikash" into "poppy-kosh!"

Aunt Chris has been making "good stuff" to eat since I was three. Like her "Poppy-Kosh Chicken," she's a peppery and colorful part of our family.

This dish is very tasty with hot cornbread!

2	tablespoons oil
1	medium onion, chopped
1	chicken, 2½ to 3 pounds, cut-up
1	large green pepper, chopped
1	tablespoon paprika
1	teaspoon salt
1	teaspoon black pepper
1	46-ounce can tomato juice
2	cups potatoes, in 1-inch cubes
1	cup elbow macaroni

1. **Heat** oil in a dutch oven, and cook onions until lightly browned.
2. **Push** onions aside; add chicken pieces and brown lightly on all sides. Add the green pepper, paprika, salt, pepper and tomato juice. Simmer chicken one hour, or until done.
3. **Cook** potatoes and macaroni in water in another pot, for 10-15 minutes, or until tender. Drain.
4. **Add** to chicken, stirring gently.

YIELD: 4-6 servings

All-Time Favorite Chicken 'N Drop Dumplin's

The centerpiece of many Southern meals is "chicken 'n dumplin's". My grandmother's rural Tennessee translation of this everyday Irish dish, features savory pieces of chicken topped with soft clouds of dumplin's in a thick, rich, golden broth. As a child, I was often served this glorious creation in a "dumplin' bowl." I still like my dumplin's in a bowl!

1	3-pound chicken or hen
¼	cup butter
1½	cups self-rising flour
1	teaspoon salt
1	egg
1	cup milk

1. **Cut** the chicken into pieces; place in a 4-quart stew pan and cover with water. Simmer until tender, about 1 hour.
2. **Remove** chicken from pot and cool. De-bone, skin and tear chicken into smaller pieces; cover and set aside.
3. **Add** butter to broth to make it richer.
4. **Remove** 1 cup broth if desired, and set aside for thinning cooked dumplin's.
5. **Mix** together flour and salt in bowl.
6. **Add** beaten egg to milk in measuring cup.
7. **Stir** egg and milk mixture into dry ingredients, just enough to moisten the flour.
8. **Bring** broth to a boil. Drop batter by teaspoonfuls into broth.
9. **Cover** tightly, and simmer gently for 15 minutes without lifting the lid, or until dumplin's are puffed and firm.
10. **Gently** fold in desired amount of chicken pieces, adding extra broth, if needed. Serve at once.

YIELD: 4-6 servings

**Left to right: 1st row,
Aunt Dot, Grandmother Mays and Tessie Mays Thompson.
2nd row,
Uncle Doug, Uncle Herbert and Uncle Edgar -- 1965.**

Crispy Southern Fried Chicken

*For my taste, this is the best chicken that has ever been served.
It should always be accompanied by Country Brown Gravy and hot
biscuits.*

2	cups flour
1	teaspoon salt
1	teaspoon garlic salt
1	teaspoon pepper
1	teaspoon paprika
2	cups buttermilk

1 cut-up chicken, 2½ to 3 pounds

cooking oil to depth of 1½ inches in heavy 10-inch skillet

1. **Combine** flour, salt, garlic salt, pepper, paprika.
2. **Pour** buttermilk in bowl.
3. **Dip** chicken pieces in buttermilk, then roll in seasoned flour
   until well coated. Let stand 10 minutes to dry coating.
4. **Start** with first piece; dip again in buttermilk and roll again in
   seasoned flour until all pieces have been dipped and rolled
   twice.
5. **Let** stand 10 minutes to dry coating.
6. **Heat** oil to 360 degrees in skillet; place chicken in hot oil,
   thicker pieces near center.
7. **Brown** on all sides over medium-high heat (be careful not to
   burn).
8. **Turn** heat down to slow simmer and cook about 25 minutes or
   until tender, turning occasionally.
9. **Drain** well on absorbent paper.

YIELD: 4 servings

Aunt Sherry's Country Brown Gravy

Aunt Sherry's gravy is lip-smackin' good to the last bite!

1. **Leave** in skillet, ½ cup of oil and browned chicken bits (in the South these are called chicken scrambles).

2. **Blend** in ½ cup flour and cook over medium heat until flour is well-browned.

3. **Add** 3 cups of warm water and 1 cup of milk, stirring briskly until well blended. Simmer gravy until thickened, adding more water or milk to thin, if desired.

4. **Add** salt and pepper to taste. Serve with fried chicken.

YIELD: 4 servings

Great-Grandmother's household hint -- To tenderize tough meat, let it soak in vinegar water for 20 minutes.

Crunchy Cornmeal Battered Chicken

My Grandmother Mays' cornmeal batter gave her chicken a flair of its own. If you are looking for a "different" fried chicken recipe, this is it.

1   **cup white cornmeal**
½   **cup flour**
1   **teaspoon salt**
½   **teaspoon pepper**
½   **teaspoon paprika**
¼   **teaspoon garlic powder**
1   **cup milk**

1   **cut-up chicken (2½ to 3 pounds)**

cooking oil to depth of 1-inch in heavy 10-inch skillet

1. **Combine** cornmeal, flour, salt, pepper, paprika and garlic powder.
2. **Place** milk in bowl.
3. **Dip** chicken pieces in milk, then roll in cornmeal mixture until well-coated. Let stand 10 minutes to dry coating.
4. **Heat** oil to medium high (360 degrees) in skillet; place chicken in hot oil, thicker pieces near center.
5. **Brown** quickly on all sides. Reduce heat, and cook about 25 minutes or until tender, turning occasionally.
6. **Drain** fried chicken on absorbent paper.

Serve immediately.

YIELD: 4 servings

Loveseat Chicken

*At **Patricia's**, in Dexter, Missouri, ladies come to lunch to enjoy special treats that they might not get during family meals. This simple to prepare version of "chicken divan" can be assembled ahead of time, so that while it bakes, you'll have time to sit on the loveseat with "him." This is a favorite with ladies, but men enjoy it, too!*

- 2 **10-ounce packages of frozen broccoli**
- 2 **cups cooked chicken, diced or 3 boneless chicken breasts, cooked and sliced**
- 2 **cups condensed cream of chicken soup**
- 1 **cup mayonnaise**
- 1 **teaspoon lemon juice**
- ½ **teaspoon curry powder**
- ½ **cup sharp process cheese, shredded**
- ½ **cup sliced almonds**

Preheat oven to 350 degrees

1. **Place** broccoli in a saucepan. Cover with water and cook until tender. Drain and arrange broccoli on bottom of 9 x 13 baking dish.
2. **Arrange** chicken on top of broccoli.
3. **Combine** soup, mayonnaise, lemon juice and curry powder, pour over chicken. Sprinkle with cheese. Top with sliced almonds.
4. **Bake** at 350 degrees for 30 minutes.

YIELD: 6-8 servings

Grandma Frances' Apple Pork Chops

These unusal pork chops are a blend of Grandma Frances' Southern cooking and Grandpa Ruben's Irish heritage, and they are delicious!

4   tablespoons oil
4   tablespoons butter
6 to 8 thick pork chops
¼   teaspoon salt
¼   teaspoon garlic salt
¼   teaspoon ground sage

2   large baking potatoes
1   teaspoon garlic salt
½   teaspoon sage

2   tart apples
¼   teaspoon cinnamon
5   tablespoons honey

4½ tablespoons flour
½   teaspoon salt
3   cups hot water

1.   **Heat** oil and butter in a large skillet .
2.   **Place** pork chops in skillet, sprinkling with ¼ teaspoon salt, garlic salt and sage.
3.   **Brown** chops and remove to 11x15-inch buttered baking dish (save pan drippings).
4.   **Peel** and thinly slice potatoes. Arrange them over chops. Sprinkle with garlic salt and sage.
5.   **Peel**, core and slice apples. Layer slices on top of potatoes. Sprinkle with cinnamon and honey.

6. **Make** sauce by adding flour and ½ teaspoon salt to drippings in skillet. Cook until brown, stirring constantly.
7. **Add** water slowly, cooking until it boils and thickens. Pour sauce over chop mixture.
8. **Cover** with foil; bake at 350 degrees for 45 minutes.
9. **Uncover** and bake for 15 minutes more, or until top is lightly browned and potatoes are tender.

YIELD: 6-8 servings

 **Great-Grandmother's beauty secret - Party Face Mask** - mix 1 egg white with 1 tablespoon honey. Apply to face and throat. When dry, remove with cool water.

Juanita's Bayou Shrimp Dish

Juanita left the Louisiana bayous with her Tennessee husband in the early 1960's, bringing this "tickle-your-taste-buds" recipe with her to the "Volunteer" state.

¼	**cup olive oil**
1	**cup chopped onion**
¾	**cup chopped celery**
2	**cups water**
1	**(15 ounce) can tomato sauce**
1	**(15 ounce) can chicken broth**
1	**teaspoon salt**
1	**teaspoon pepper**
2	**garlic cloves, minced**
	dash of cayenne pepper
3	**pounds shelled and cleaned shrimp**

1. **Heat** olive oil (not to hot or it will burn) in large pot. Saute, onion and celery in oil until soft.
2. **Add** water, tomato sauce, chicken broth, salt, pepper, garlic and cayenne.
3. **Cover** kettle and simmer 30 minutes.
4. **Add** shrimp. Cook, just until shrimp are uniformly pink and cooked through, about 10-15 minutes. Do not overcook.

Serve in bowls over boiled rice or Rice Lyonnaise.

YIELD: 4-6 servings

Rice Lyonnaise

¾ cup onion, chopped
4   tablespoons butter
3   cups hot cooked rice
¼ cup pimento peppers, diced

1. **In** a non-stick skillet, sauté, onions in butter until tender.
2. **Add** rice and pimento peppers. Cook over low heat until rice is golden, stirring occasionally.

YIELD: 4-6 servings

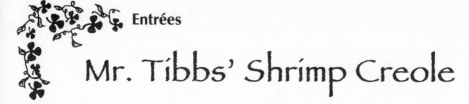

Mr. Tibbs' Shrimp Creole

*Jennifer Hazel, sous-chef of the **Royal N'Orleans Restaurant**, in Cape Girardeau, Missouri -- on the Mississippi River -- has adapted this from from an original 1954 recipe by Mr. Tibbs. Tibbs was one of the restaurant's early cooks.*

BASIC SAUCE:

¼	cup pork fat
1	large onion, chopped
½	large stalk of celery, minced
1	medium carrot, chopped
5	pounds fresh tomatoes
1	cup tomato sauce
¼	teaspoon white pepper
¼	teaspoon black pepper
¼	teaspoon cayenne pepper
3	tablespoons instant coffee
1	teaspoon dried sweet basil
1	teaspoon dried thyme
1	bay leaf
3	tablespoons sugar
	Tabasco sauce to taste

1. **Sauté**, onions in pork fat in a large pot over low heat, until transparent. Add celery and carrots and cook until soft, but not mushy.
2. **Add** fresh tomatoes, tomato sauce, peppers and coffee. Bring to a boil.
3. **Stir** in basil, thyme, sugar and Tabasco sauce. Reduce heat to simmer and cook until all vegetables are tender.

   YIELD: enough for 8 servings

Shrimp Creole--
Per Person

8   jumbo shrimp, deveined and peeled
2   cups Basic Sauce
2   tablespoons onion, chopped
¼   cup fresh mushrooms
1   ounce sherry, if desired
1   cup cooked white rice

1. **Combine** shrimp and 2 cups of basic sauce in saucepan. Cook over high heat until shrimp are almost cooked through. Add onions, mushrooms and sherry. Simmer until shrimp are cooked through.
2. **Serve** over white rice.

YIELD: 1 serving

"Real" Men Brunch Casserole

*Patty Shell of **Patricia's Tea Room** began her food service career seventeen years ago in Essex, Missouri, with two friends, Pat and Karen, in Unique Catering. Preparing large quantities of brunch foods for those special occasions meant preparing food ahead of time for last minute baking. The following brunch casserole is great for large groups. Just double or triple, keep on adding -- just get a big enough baking pan. Make sure you allow extra cooking time for the larger batches, and allow some sitting time from the oven to your table.*

In Southeast Missouri, along the Mississippi, it is sometimes hard to please men with a "specialty" like this, but this casserole is one that "real" men will eat with gusto.

6	eggs, beaten
1¾	cups milk
7	slices white bread, cubed and crustless
⅛	teaspoon salt
1	teaspoon dry mustard
1	pound hot sausage, cooked and drained
1	cup cheddar cheese, grated
1	cup cheddar cheese, grated (to garnish casserole after baking)

1. **Combine** first seven ingredients in order given and pour into 2-quart lightly greased casserole dish. Refrigerate overnight.
2. **Remove** casserole from refrigerator the next morning. (If casserole dish cannot go directly from cold refrigerator to hot oven, let stand to room temperature.
3. **Bake** at 350 degrees for 45 minutes or until golden brown.
4. **Top** with 1 cup grated cheddar cheese. Let sit for 5 to 10 minutes before serving.

   YIELD: 6 servings

Broccoli & Crab Casserole

This delicious casserole is served on Sunday and holiday buffets at **Rosie's Bar & Grille**, *in New Madrid, Missouri.*

12   slices of white bread, crusts removed
2½   cups milk
1   cup mayonnaise
2   10-ounce packages frozen, chopped broccoli
1   pound fresh regular or imitation crab
½   cup onion, chopped
½   teaspoon salt
¼   teaspoon pepper
1   cup cheddar cheese, grated

Preheat oven to 350 degrees

1. **Cut** bread into ½-inch cubes and place in a large bowl. Add milk and mayonnaise, mix well, cover and refrigerate for 30 minutes.
2. **Cook** broccoli according to package directions; drain. Grease a 9 x 13-inch baking dish with butter; layer cooked and drained broccoli in bottom of pan.
3. **Cut** crab into small pieces in a bowl. Add onion, salt and pepper. Combine crab mixture with bread mixture, mixing well and spoon bread-crab mixture over broccoli.
4. **Bake**, uncovered, at 350 degrees for 40 minutes.
5. **Sprinkle** cheese over top and cook for additional 5 minutes or until cheese melts. Cool 10 minutes before serving.

YIELD: 6 servings

Notes

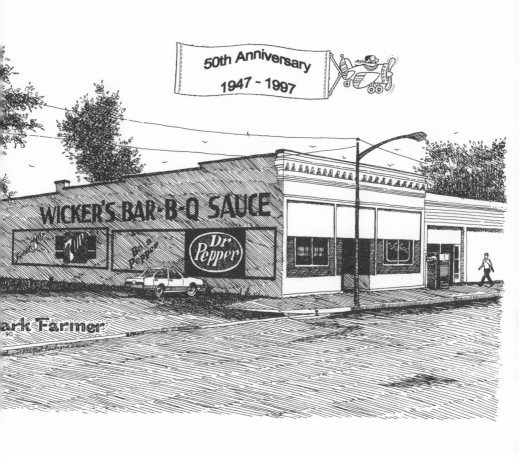

50th Anniversary
1947 - 1997

WICKER'S BAR-B-Q SAUCE

Dr Pepper

ark Farmer

Food Products, Inc.

Presents

Favorite Wicker's Recipes

WICKER'S CELEBRATES 50 YEARS OF GREAT BARBECUE

When old Peck Wicker cooked up some barbecue, down in the Missouri Bootheel, people would come from miles around. Each weekend, from May to October, Peck would set up an open pit and cook nearly a ton of meat basted with his special sauce. And, he'd sell it all.

That was 50 years ago!

Today, Wicker's is still made using Peck's secret formula of peppers and spices in a vinegar base. Containing no sugar, tomatoes or oil— Wicker's® Original Barbecue Marinade & Baste tenderizes and imparts a wonderful, mildly spicy flavor.

The Wicker's plant, located in the center of the little town of Hornersville, Missouri (Pop. 629), turns out cases and cases of the famous baste each week — along with Wicker's Thicker, a pour-on table sauce; Wicker's Gourmet Steak Sauce; and Wicker's Lite Low-Sodium — the same great baste, with 50% less sodium.

Wicker's is as popular with locals as it is with chefs, Memphis in May World Championship Barbecue Cooking Contest teams, and homesick folks who remember its great taste and mail-order it from places as far away as New York and Canada.

Wicker's is delicious on beef, pork, chicken and fish. It's also a great shrimp boil and seasoning in tomato juice, Bloody Marys, Baked Beans and Chili. Best of all, Wicker's is 100% natural. Look for it in your local market, or call 1-800-847-0032 for information on store locations, mail-ordering, gift packs, t-shirts, hats, aprons, and other items. (Visa and MasterCard accepted.)

In the words of Peck Wicker, "Wicker's is the taste sensation beyond imagination!"

WICKER'S® FOOD PRODUCTS, INC.
301 N. Mound Street
Hornersville, Missouri 63855
1-800-847-0032

"Wickered" Baked Beans

Wicker's® Original Barbecue Marinade & Baste, a vinegary concoction of peppers and spices, was invented and is still made in the little town of Hornersville, Missouri (Pop. 629). Added to beans, Wicker's gives them a mildly spicy jolt -- just perfect with barbecued pork or chicken.

4	16-ounce cans pork & beans
¼	pound lean bacon, diced
1	large onion, diced
2	cloves garlic, minced
	pepper, to taste
	Worcestershire sauce, to taste
⅓	cup brown sugar, packed
½	cup catsup
½	cup Wicker's® Original Barbecue Marinade & Baste

Preheat oven to 325 degrees

1. **Open** the beans and pour away excess liquid at top of each can.
2. **Sauté**, bacon and onions, until bacon is half- cooked.
3. **Add** beans and remaining ingredients, stirring to blend well.
4. **Pour** into 2-quart open casserole dish. Bake at 325 degrees for 40 minutes or until bubbly and edges are brown.

YIELD: 12 servings

Wickered Holiday Cornbread

"Wicker's" is not only great for marinating and basting -- it adds "zip" to this yummy cornbread.

1   cup yellow cornmeal
1   cup all-purpose flour
1   teaspoon baking powder
½   teaspoon baking soda
    pinch of salt
4   ounces shredded cheddar cheese
    one small onion, diced
½   green bell pepper, diced fine
½   red bell pepper, diced fine
2   eggs
½   cup milk
½   cup Wicker's® Original Barbecue Marinade & Baste
2   tablespoons vegetable oil

1. **Mix** together first nine ingredients.
2. **Blend** eggs, milk and Wicker's and add, stirring to form batter.
3. **Swirl** vegetable oil in 10-inch iron skillet over medium-high heat until very hot, but not smoking.
4. **Pour** oil into batter, blend; pour batter back into skillet.
5. **Bake** about 25 minutes, or until puffed and brown.
6. **Cool** slightly and cut into wedges.

YIELD: 8-10 servings

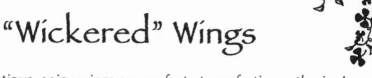

"Wickered" Wings

These scrumptious, spicy wings are perfect at any festive gathering!

2   **dozen chicken wings**
1   **28-ounce bottle Wicker's® Original Barbecue Marinade & Baste**

    celery sticks
    blue cheese dressing
    hot sauce, if desired

Preheat oven to 325 degrees

1. **Cut** wings in half to make 48 pieces, reserving tips for stock or another use.
2. **Marinate** wing pieces at room temperature in 1 cup Wicker's for 1-2 hours, or overnight in the refrigerator.
3. **Drain** wings and place in glass or enameled pan. Cover with 1 cup Wicker's and bake, basting frequently until wings are dark brown and coated with spices, about 45 minutes. Add more Wicker's as needed, if pan juices run dry.
4. **Serve** with celery sticks, blue cheese dressing and hot sauce, if desired.

YIELD: 6-8 servings

Wickered Pork Shoulder

Here's a great way to make a pork "butt" or shoulder anytime of year. This melt-in-your mouth roast is great sliced— for Sunday dinner— or chopped for weekday sandwiches. Chill the "pot likker", remove the fat, and you'll have a savory sauce.

1   **5-6 pound pork butt or shoulder**
3-4 **cloves fresh garlic, cut in slivers**
1   **onion, sliced**
1   **28-oz bottle Wicker's® Original Barbecue Marinade & Baste**

1.   **Trim** as much fat as possible from the pork roast. Insert the garlic slivers all over, and place roast in a dutch oven or heavy iron pot with lid.
2.   **Shake** up the bottle of Wicker's Original and pour half of it over the meat. Top with sliced onion. Cover tightly and bake in a 325 degree oven for about 2-3 hours, basting with pan juices and turning occasionally, until the meat is fork tender. Add more Wicker's® if pot becomes dry.
3.   **Remove** meat from pot and let stand a few minutes before carving.

YIELD: 8-10 servings

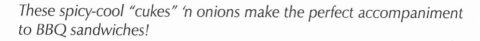

Spicy Wickered
Cucumbers & Onions

These spicy-cool "cukes" 'n onions make the perfect accompaniment to BBQ sandwiches!

3	**medium cucumbers**
3	**medium onions (preferably Vidalia or sweet red onions)**
2	**cups Wicker's® Original Barbecue Marinade & Baste**

Peel and thinly slice cucumbers and onions. Pour 2 cups of Wicker's over cucumbers and onions; cover and marinate in refrigerator at least 1 hour. Drain before serving.

Notes

River Birch Mall

River Birch Antique Gallery

Presents

Cakes
and
Frostings

RIVER BIRCH MALL

The **River Birch Mall**, formerly Kingsway Plaza, in Sikeston, Missouri, was purchased by Larry and Brenda DeWitt in 1993 at a time when the community thought that the property had seen its brightest days. *Built in 1970, this mall was the only one of its kind between St. Louis, Missouri and Memphis, Tennessee.*

DeWitt, a horticulturist and landscape designer, who believed the mall could be revitalized, formulated the concept for its new image. He named it *River Birch* after the river birch tree, which is beautiful year 'round and known for its resistance to disease and tolerance to the local climate. It was also Larry's favorite tree for use in landscaping designs.

Plans are now underway for an interior and exterior renovation, utilizing the trees as a focus of the design. Increased retail growth in the vicinity of **River Birch Mall** and its location near I-57 and I-55 highways, make it a prime choice for specialty stores. Housing over 30 businesses, **River Birch Mall** is a must for both tourists and local shoppers. Come and spend a day ... you'll be glad you did!

* RIVER BIRCH MALL *

Artistically Inclined

Heavenly Brew Gourmet Coffee Shop

River Birch Antique Gallery

901 S. Kingshighway
Sikeston, Missouri 63869
573-472-4700

From I-55 take Exit 66B to Hwy. 61, then North to Kingshighway.

Mother's Cadillac Strawberry Cake

If cakes were cars, this one would be a Cadillac - a shiny red one!

1   **box yellow cake mix**
1   **box strawberry Jello**
4   **eggs**
¼   **cup water**
¼   **cup oil**
1   **cup sliced strawberries, fresh or frozen**

Preheat oven to 350 degrees.

1. **Combine** all ingredients, in order given; mix well.
2. **Pour** into three greased and floured 9-inch layer pans; or a 9 x 13-inch baking pan; or large tube pan. Bake in 350 degree oven until done, or when knife inserted into center comes out clean.
3. **Cool** cake for 15 minutes, remove from pan(s) and frost with Strawberry Frosting (p.124).

YIELD: 8-10 servings

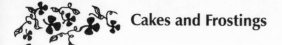

DEBBIE AND THE WHITE FROSTING

To say the least, Debbie was not a cook. To say the most, she should have been banished from the kitchen. But, every so often, she would convince herself that if everyone else could cook, so could she. This was always a faulty assumption on her part, and one summer afternoon, in 1967, she created the monster frosting.

When I answered my telephone that afternoon, there was Debbie's frantic voice mumbling something about being attacked by white frosting! Suddenly, I was standing in her kitchen stunned that two egg whites could have covered everything-- including Debbie. Apparently, Debbie and the mixer had fought -- and the mixer won!

I noticed the mixer on the counter, but saw no beaters. When I asked where the beaters were, Debbie pointed to the double boiler still sitting on the burner. To my amazement, the beaters were standing upright in the frosting. All the king's horses and all the king's men could not remove those beaters from the frosting, nor the frosting from that double boiler!

What went wrong that afternoon is inexplicable, for Debbie was using my Grandmother Mays' white frosting recipe, and it is one of the best (and easiest!) frostings I've ever made. Now, whenever I make it, laughter and happy memories of Debbie fill my kitchen.

Grandmother Mays' White Frosting

2   egg whites
1   cup light corn syrup
8   tablespoons marshmallow cream
½   teaspoon pure vanilla extract

1.   **Place** egg whites and corn syrup in top of double boiler over simmering water.
2.   **Beat** with a hand-held mixer or rotary beater until fluffy.
3.   **Add** marshmallow cream and vanilla extract; beat until stiff.
4.   **Spread** over cooled cake.

   YIELD: enough for a 9 x 13-inch or 2-layer cake

Dianne's Mississippi Mud Cake

My friend, Dianne Compton, has developed "the" premier recipe for Mississippi Mud Cake. Fortunately, she has agreed to share it with you and me.

2   cups sugar
1   cup vegetable oil
4   eggs
1½ cups self-rising flour
⅓   cup cocoa
1   teaspoon pure vanilla extract
1   cup chopped pecans
1   7-ounce jar marshmallow cream

Preheat oven to 350 degrees.

1.   **Grease** and flour a 9 x 13-inch or 11 x 15-inch baking pan.
2.   **Cream** together sugar and oil.
3.   **Add** eggs one at a time, beating mixture by hand.
4.   **Sift** together flour and cocoa and add to above, mixing well.
5.   **Add** vanilla extract and pecans.
6.   **Bake** at 350 degrees for 30 minutes or until done.
7.   **Spread** marshmallow cream over top, while hot.
8.   **Top** marshmallow cream with Mississippi Mud icing (p.124).

YIELD: 10-12 servings

Aunt Dottie's Best-Ever Chocolate Loaf Cake

My Aunt Dottie says, "This cake, cooks quick and goes fast".

½ **cup vegetable shortening**
1 **cup sugar**
1 **egg**
½ **cup milk**
1 **teaspoon pure vanilla extract**
1½ **cups self-rising flour**
    dash of salt
½ **cup boiling water**
½ **cup cocoa powder**

Preheat oven to 325 degrees.

1. **Cream** shortening and sugar together.
2. **Add** egg and blend well.
3. **Blend** in milk and vanilla extract.
4. **Add** flour and salt, mix well.
5. **Dissolve** cocoa in boiling water. Add to flour mixture.
6. **Pour** into 9 x 5-inch, well-greased loaf pan. Bake for 30 minutes, or until wooden pick inserted in center comes out clean.
7. **Cool** for 15 minutes, then remove from pan. Finish cooling on rack.

YIELD: 8-10 servings

NOTE: If desired, top loaf with sifted, powdered sugar before serving.

Extraordinary Pumpkin Cake

This recipe takes pumpkin to new heights. Is it any wonder that it's my family's favorite Thanksgiving dinner dessert!

4 **eggs, lightly beaten**
1 **20-ounce can solid-pack pumpkin**
1½ **cups sugar**
1 **teaspoon cinnamon**
1 **teaspoon salt**
1 **12-ounce can Milnot**
1 **18-ounce package yellow cake mix**
1 **cup butter, melted**
1 **cup chopped pecans**

Preheat oven to 325 degrees.

1. **Mix** eggs, pumpkin, sugar, cinnamon, salt and Milnot in order given. Pour into ungreased 9 x 13-inch pan.
2. **Sprinkle** cake mix over pumpkin filling. Pour melted butter over cake mix. Sprinkle with pecans.
3. **Bake** at 325 degrees for 1 to 1¼ hours, or until knife inserted into center comes out clean.
4. **Leave** cake in pan. Serve warm or cold, plain or with whipped cream. I like to top it with Hot Butter Sauce (p.125).

YIELD: 10-12 servings

Lura Dell's Missouri Apple Cake

"Moist and tender with a honey glaze" is the way my husband remembers his grandmother's fresh apple cake. Lurie Dell made apple cakes and Sunday dinner until she was almost ninety.

2	**cups sugar**
1½	**cups corn oil**
3	**eggs**
3	**cups diced apples**
1	**teaspoon cinnamon**
3	**cups self-rising flour**
½	**teaspoon baking soda**
1	**teaspoon pure vanilla extract**
¼	**teaspoon pure almond extract**

Preheat oven to 350 degrees.

1. **Grease** and flour a 9 x 13-inch baking pan.
2. **Mix** sugar and oil in large bowl. Beat well.
3. **Beat** in eggs, one at time.
4. **Toss** diced apples with cinnamon and add to mixture.
5. **Mix** flour and baking soda, add one cup at a time blending well.
6. **Stir** in extracts and mix well. Batter will be very thick.
7. **Bake** in prepared pan for 45 minutes, or until done.
8. **Serve** with Honey Glaze (p.125).

YIELD: 12 servings

Sarah Lucresia's
Sweetheart Butter Cake

I am sharing with the readers of this book -- a one-hundred-twenty-five year-old family tradition -- the passing on of Sarah Lucresia's cherished butter cake recipe.

Sarah Lucresia Turner, the great-grandmother of Angie Holtzhouser, made her "Sweetheart Butter Cake" from a recipe brought to this country by her French grandmother.

Sarah Lucresia, a tall, slim, dark-haired French girl, won the heart of Charlie Turner, a short, round, blond Irishman, in 1900, with her delicious "Sweetheart Butter Cake".

Their treasured thirty-year marriage produced eight beloved children. Sarah Lucresia died in 1930, but she walked in the heart and soul of Charlie Turner until his death in 1960.

Since this "Sweetheart Butter Cake" is my husband Larry Joe's favorite, I make it to remind him of who and what won his heart.

Charlie and Sarah Lucresia Turner - 1930

Sarah Lucresia's "Sweetheart Butter Cake" recipe was passed from Sarah Lucresia Turner to Ondeen Turner Mays to Tessie Mays Thompson, to Angie Thompson Potter Holtzhouser, and to Johnna Fourthman Potter -- the woman who walks in my son Rick's heart-- so that it can forever be passed on to the next generation, to continue winning hearts.

Ellie Potter, our sixth generation, was born on November 22, 1995. She, too, will one day win hearts with "Sarah Lucresia's Sweetheart Butter Cake".

I use an electric mixer when making this cake.

1	**pound unsalted butter, at room temperature**
2	**cups sugar**
7	**eggs**
¼	**cup heavy cream**
1	**teaspoon pure vanilla extract**
3	**cups self-rising flour**

Preheat oven to 350 degrees.

1. **Cream** softened butter and sugar together.
2. **Add** eggs one at a time, beating well after each addition.
3. **Add** cream and vanilla, beating well.
4. **Add** flour one cup at a time, beating well. This makes a very thick batter.
5. **Bake** in a large, well-greased bundt pan at 350 degrees for 15 minutes. Reduce heat to 325 degrees and continue baking for another 45 minutes, or until an inserted knife blade comes out clean.
6. **Place** bundt pan on cooling rack for 15 minutes; then loosen edges of cake with a sharp knife. Invert onto a large cake plate.

Cake can be served plain, iced or with fresh fruit.

YIELD: 12 servings

Phyllis' Carrot Cake

This delectable carrot cake is a favorite of Phyllis Cline's, proprietor of **Forty Carrots***, gourmet shop and cooking school, in Memphis, Tennessee.*

4   eggs
1½ cups vegetable oil
1   small can crushed pineapple, undrained
1   cup sugar
1   cup brown sugar
½   teaspoon cinnamon
¼   teaspoon cardamom
¼   teaspoon nutmeg
2   cups all-purpose flour
2   teaspoons baking powder
2   scant teaspoons baking soda
1   teaspoon salt
3   cups raw carrots, grated

Preheat oven to 300 degrees

1. **Combine** wet ingredients: eggs, oil and pineapple in a large bowl.
2. **Sift** together dry ingredients: sugar, brown sugar, cinnamon, cardamon, nutmeg, flour, baking powder, baking soda and salt in a separate bowl. Add carrots.
3. **Blend** dry mixture into wet mixture.
4. **Pour** batter into a greased and floured 10 x 10 pan. Bake at 300 degrees for 35-45 minutes, or until cake tests done.
5. **Cool** 15 minutes in pan. Remove from pan and finish cooling on rack. When cool, frost with Cream Cheese Frosting (p. 126).

YIELD: 8 servings

Fresh Coconut Cake

*When ladies dine at **Patricia's Tea Room** in Dexter, Missouri, they are always out for a special "TREAT". And, of course, deliciously sinful desserts, like this one, are high on the priority list. Some ladies even look at the dessert menu first at Patricia's-- before making their entrée selections. This fresh coconut cake looks s-o-o elegant on a pretty cake stand, but yet, it can be made easily for those special occasions at home.*

1	18½-ounce box white pudding cake mix
2	cups sugar
2	cups sour cream
2	9-ounce packages frozen coconut, thawed
1	large tub Cool Whip, thawed

Preheat oven to 350 degrees

1. **Bake** cake as directed on box, using 2 8-inch cake pans. Cool.
2. **Combine** sugar, sour cream and coconut and chill.
3. **Split** each layer in half. Reserve 1 cup sour cream mixture for frosting. Spread remainder between layers of cake.
4. **Combine** reserved sour cream mixture with Cool Whip. Blend until smooth. Spread on top and sides of cake. Be very generous with frosting on sides and top of cake. (You might even want to double filling and frosting recipe.)

YIELD: 8-10 servings

NOTE: This cake is even better if allowed to sit in refrigerator for 3 days before serving...but who can wait!!!??

Strawberry Frosting

1   8-ounce package cream cheese
4   tablespoons unsalted butter
1   cup powdered sugar
1   cup sliced strawberries, fresh or frozen

1. **Melt** cream cheese and butter together, over low heat. Add powdered sugar and stir well. Remove from heat.
2. **Fold** in strawberries and blend well. If thicker frosting is desired, add more powdered sugar.
3. **Use** as filling and frosting for Mother's Cadillac Strawberry Cake (p. 113).

YIELD: About 3 cups of frosting

Mississippi Mud Icing

2   sticks butter, melted
½   cup cocoa
1   16-ounce box powdered sugar
½   cup evaporated milk
1   teaspoon pure vanilla extract
1   cup chopped pecans

1. **Sift** cocoa and sugar together, add to melted butter -- stir until well blended.
2. **Add** evaporated milk, vanilla extract and pecans.
3. **Icing** will be thin. Pour over marshmallow cream on Dianne's Mississippi Mud Cake (p. 116).
4. **Let** it set several hours or overnight before serving.

YIELD: about 3 cups of icing

Hot Butter Sauce

1 stick butter
1 cup sugar
½ cup evaporated milk
½ teaspoon pure vanilla extract

1. **Combine** butter, sugar and cream in small saucepan. Cook over medium heat until thickened, stirring often.
2. **Stir** in vanilla extract. Pour over Extraordinary Pumpkin Cake (p. 118) while still hot.

YIELD: 1½ cups of sauce

Honey Glaze

4 tablespoons honey
¾ cup sugar
½ cup cream
½ cup butter

1. **Combine** all ingredients in pan and heat over low heat, stirring constantly, until hot and sugar melts.
2. **Pour** over Lurie Dell's Missouri Apple Cake (p. 119). May be poured over whole cake or individual slices.

YIELD: 2 cups of glaze

World War II White Frosting

During World War II, powdered sugar was even harder to come by than granulated, white sugar. This fluffy frosting needs no powdered sugar.

1	cup milk
4	tablespoons flour
½	cup unsalted butter
1	cup sugar

1. **Boil** milk and flour over low heat till thick; set aside until very cool.
2. **Cream** together butter and sugar.
3. **Whip** all ingredients with electric mixer until frosting becomes fluffy. Spread on cake.

YIELD: enough for one 8-9-inch square cake

Cream Cheese Frosting

1	pound confectioner's sugar
1	8-ounce package cream cheese, softened
½	stick butter, softened
1	teaspoon vanilla extract

1. **Combine** all ingredients in a large bowl and beat with an electric mixer until smooth and fluffy.
2. **Frost** cake when cool.

YIELD: 3 cups

The
Blue Owl

Restaurant
and
Bakery

in
Historic Kimmswick, Missouri

Presents

Pies

THE BLUE OWL RESTAURANT AND BAKERY

The Blue Owl Restaurant and Bakery in Historic Kimmswick, Missouri is famous for hearty breakfasts, country-style lunches and fabulous desserts served on old English China. The quaint and charming atmosphere, the warm and friendly service, as well as delicious home cooking makes for an unforgettable dining experience.

The Blue Owl Bakery is one of a kind, featuring over 100 different choices for dessert – homemade pies with tender, flaky crusts, bubbling hot from the oven, assorted specialty cakes, luscious cheesecakes, pastries, cookies, candies and sugar-free desserts for those who can't indulge in sugar! Choose from an assortment of American favorites or European delicacies, baked fresh daily and made with only the finest ingredients.

You can enjoy dining on Ms. Mary's Veranda, year round. **The Blue Owl** features seasonal live music on the veranda including an accordion player, dulcimer player and a button-box player.

Owner Mary Hostetter and her staff will welcome you and invite you to share in the experience of a wonderful meal in a setting "just like home."

The Blue Owl Restaurant and Bakery

2nd and Mill Street
Kimmswick, Missouri 63053
314-464-3128

With pride and the commitment to provide quality, fresh food, a warm atmosphere, and an extraordinary dining experience to every customer.

Never-Fail Meringue

3 egg whites
½ teaspoon cream of tartar
6 tablespoons powdered sugar
2 tablespoons marshmallow cream
½ teaspoon pure vanilla extract

1. **Preheat** oven to 350 degrees (325 degrees, if oven cooks hot).
2. **Whip** egg whites until frothy.
3. **Add** cream of tartar. Whip until stiff (peaks will lean over slightly when beaters are removed).
4. **Beat** in marshmallow cream.
5. **Beat** in powdered sugar 2 tablespoons at a time.
6. **Beat** in vanilla extract.
7. **Spread** on pie, making sure to seal edges around crust and bake 10 to 15 minutes, or until lightly-browned.

YIELD: Enough meringue for 9-inch pie

Arnell's Coconut Cream Pie

Arnell Mitchell was my Mother's best friend and a superb cook. For years she made all the desserts for the local cafe, in the small southern town where I grew up.

While all her desserts were great, Arnell was famous for her coconut pies. They were a confection of vanilla cream, moist fresh coconut and mounds of "just-rightly" browned meringue nestled in a tender crust. Arnell's Coconut Cream Pie was the most requested dessert on the menu.

One baked deep-dish 9" pie crust (cooled)

1½ cups sugar
4   tablespoons cornstarch
½   teaspoon salt
2   cups of milk
3   egg yolks (save the whites for the meringue)
1   teaspoon pure vanilla extract
4   tablespoons butter
1   cup fresh or frozen grated coconut

1. **Mix** sugar, cornstarch and salt in top of double boiler or heavy saucepan.
2. **Combine** milk and egg yolks and add to sugar mixture. Cook, stirring, over simmering water until thickened.
3. **Remove** from heat, add vanilla extract and butter; stir until butter melts.
4. **Add** coconut, mixing well.
5. **Pour** into prepared pie shell.
6. **Top** with meringue and brown lightly. (See recipe on page 129)

YIELD: 6 servings.

My Daddy's Favorite Pecan Pie

"All-by-myself," at age 10, I made my first pecan pie as a surprise for my Daddy. It's still his favorite.

1   cup sugar
1   tablespoon flour
3   tablespoons butter, melted
3   eggs slightly beaten
½   teaspoon pure vanilla extract
1   cup white corn syrup
1   cup pecan pieces
1   prepared unbaked 9-inch pie crust

Preheat oven to 375 degrees.

1. **Mix** sugar and flour.
2. **Add** butter, eggs and vanilla to sugar mixture. Blend well.
3. **Add** syrup, mix well.
4. **Line** pie crust with pecan pieces.
5. **Pour** syrup mixture over pecan pieces.
6. **Bake** at 375 degrees for 15 minutes. Reduce heat to 350 degrees and bake for 30 minutes more, or until the center is firm to the touch and the crust is lightly browned.
7. **Cool** on rack for 1 hour before serving.

YIELD: 6-8 servings.

BEGGAR AND THE COOKIES

It was a bright, sunny afternoon at Tan-Tar-A Estates, at the Lake of the Ozarks in Missouri, in 1989. My husband and I were enjoying the view from our sixth-floor balcony shortly after our arrival. It was then that I spied a frisky squirrel on the ground, swiftly nipping the buds from a flower bed. I shouted at him that he was not being a good boy! To our surprise, he stopped his bud nipping and looked right up at us. I showed him a cookie, and, again, began talking to him. In a flash, he came straight up the rocky corner of the building onto the railing of our balcony. We left him a vanilla cookie, and when we backed away, Beggar, the squirrel, came onto the balcony and retrieved the cookie.

The next morning, before leaving for the day, we left vanilla cookies and OREO* cookies on the balcony for Beggar. When we returned, the vanilla cookies were still there, but the OREO cookies were gone! After that morning, Beggar would eat nothing but OREO cookies.

Beggar came morning and evening during our week's stay. If we gave him a stack of OREO cookies, he would work and tug to get them apart, eating the filling while carrying a "shell" with him for later.

If Beggar came to the balcony and found no Oreo cookies, he would peer into the patio door to get our attention. Of course, then he got all the OREO cookies he wanted! For many years to come, we will smile when we recall Beggar sitting there with OREO cookies and cream on his devilish little face!

*OREO Chocolate Sandwich Cookies is a registered trademark of Nabisco.

Chocolate Cookie Crust Pie

36 OREO cookies
1 stick unsalted butter, melted
2 8-ounce packages cream cheese, at room temperature
2 cans Eagle brand condensed milk
1 16-ounce jar chocolate fudge sauce
1 8-ounce container of Cool Whip

1. **Crush** OREO cookies in a sealed plastic bag with a rolling pin. Spoon crumbs into a 9 x 13-inch pan, and spread evenly.
2. **Melt** butter and pour over crushed cookies. Freeze for 15 minutes.
3. **Beat** softened cream cheese in medium bowl until light and fluffy.
4. **Add** condensed milk to cheese, and mix until smooth.
5. **Pour** over cookie mixture. Refrigerate until firm, about one hour.
6. **Pour** chocolate sauce over cream cheese mixture. Refrigerate for 30 minutes.
7. **Top** with Cool Whip.
8. **Refrigerate** for at least six hours before serving.

YIELD: 8-10 servings

Grandmother Mays' Lemon Cream Pie

My Grandmother Mays' kitchen was filled with good things to eat. Country bacon and breakfast biscuits were waiting for you in the warming compartment of the stove, while her cupboard stored sweet dried fruits from the summer harvest. In my whole life, Grandmother Mays' cookie jar was never empty. But, my favorite spot was her old pie safe, for there was always a "Lemon Cream Pie" just waiting for me. Seated on the wooden bench at her table, I would devour this velvety concoction of cream and lemon in its perfect crispy crust, topped with mile-high meringue.

1½ **cups sugar**
5   **tablespoons flour**
1   **cup evaporated milk**
½   **cup milk**
½   **cup fresh lemon juice**
4   **egg yolks (reserve 3 egg whites for meringue)**
1   **baked 9-inch deep-dish pie crust**

Preheat oven to 325 degrees.

1. **Mix** sugar and flour in a heavy saucepan .
2. **Add** both milks and lemon juice; stir well.
3. **Whisk** in egg yolks.
4. **Cook** mixture, over low heat, until boiling point is reached and custard has thickened, stirring constantly, about 10 minutes.
5. **Stir** in butter.
6. **Pour** hot filling into baked pie shell.
7. **Spread** meringue over filling and bake in preheated 325 degree oven for 10 to 15 minutes until lightly browned. See meringue recipe on page 129.
8. **Cool** pie on rack for 2 hours before serving.

YIELD: 6-8 servings.

Lloyd's Sunny Pineapple Pie

This pie, an adventure in tart and sweet, is one of my cousin Lloyd's favorites. For Lloyd, the adventurer, who calls the sunny west his home, but travels all over the world, this pie always brings him back to his childhood.

FILLING:

1   cup sugar
¼   cup flour
¼   teaspoon salt
1   tablespoon lemon juice
2   tablespoons butter, melted
1   20-ounce can crushed pineapple in its own juice; drained, reserving liquid for glaze
2   unbaked 9-inch pie crusts

GLAZE:

1   tablespoon butter, softened
½   cup powdered sugar
2   tablespoons reserved pineapple liquid

Preheat oven to 375 degrees.

1. **Combine** all filling ingredients in order given in a large bowl, mix well.
2. **Spread** over bottom of pie crust-lined pan.
3. **Top** with second crust; seal edges and flute. Cut slits in top crust.
4. **Bake** at 375 degrees for 35 minutes or until golden brown.
5. **Combine** glaze ingredients, adding enough pineapple liquid for an easy spreading consistency. Drizzle or spread glaze over top of hot pie.
6. **Cool** on rack for 1 hour before serving.

YIELD: 6-8 servings.

Aunt Susan's St. Louis Raisin Pie

Raisin pie hàs a touch of Ireland in it, for the Irish throw a handful of raisins into many breads and desserts. My Aunt Susan does the Irish tradition justice with this recipe.

2　cups raisins, dark or light
2　cups water
2　tablespoons cornstarch
¼　cup cold water
1　teaspoon cinnamon
1　tablespoon white vinegar
½　cup brown sugar, packed
⅛　teaspoon salt
1　tablespoon butter
1　prepared 9-inch pie crust

Preheat oven to 425 degrees.

1.　**Boil** raisins in 2 cups water for 5 minutes, remove from heat.
2.　**Dissolve** cornstarch in ¼ cup water and add to raisin mixture, mixing well.
3.　**Add** cinnamon, vinegar, brown sugar, salt and butter, blending well.
4.　**Pour** mixture into prepared crust and bake at 425 degrees for 25 minutes or until lightly browned.

YIELD: 6-8 servings.

Tessie's Old-South Chess Pie

A piece of chess pie is a piece of rich, Southern tradition, and my Mother makes the best chess pies using this treasured family recipe.

1½ cups sugar
2 tablespoons flour
1 stick unsalted butter, melted
½ cup evaporated milk
3 eggs, lightly beaten
1 prepared unbaked 9-inch pie crust

Preheat oven to 325 degrees.

1. **Mix** sugar and flour.
2. **Add** melted butter to mixture.
3. **Blend** in evaporated milk.
4. **Add** eggs, mix well.
5. **Pour** into prepared crust.
6. **Bake** at 325 degrees for 1 hour or until center is firm to the touch.
7. **Cool** on rack 1 hour before serving.

YIELD: 6-8 servings.

Levee-High Apple Pie

The Blue Owl Restaurant and Bakery, located near the Mississippi River in Kimmswick, Missouri, created this pie to resemble the earthen levee which saved the entire town from the ravaging floodwaters of the Great Flood of '93.

12	cups Granny Smith apples, peeled and thinly sliced
1	cup sugar
¼	cup flour
2	teaspoons ground cinnamon
	dash of salt
1	tablespoon butter
1	tablespoon sugar
¼	cup milk
2	deep-dish pie crusts, unbaked (p. 139)

Preheat oven to 450 degrees.

1. **Combine** apples, sugar, flour, cinnamon and salt.
2. **Arrange** bottom crust in pie plate, letting dough hang slightly over edges.
3. **Mound** apples by using a small, deep mixing bowl for mold. Invert filled bowl into deep dish pie crust. Dot apples with butter.
4. **Cover** mounded apples with top crust. Moisten, seal, and flute edges of crust tightly. Brush top with a small amount of milk and sugar mixed together. Prick crust to allow steam to escape.
5. **Bake** at 450 degrees for 15 minutes, then reduce heat to 350 degrees and bake for 1 hour, or until crust is golden brown.

YIELD: 8 servings

Deep Dish Pie Crust

1½ cups all-purpose flour
¾ teaspoon salt
⅓ cup + 2 tablespoons butter-flavored Crisco
5 tablespoons cold water

1. **Cut** flour into Crisco. Add salt and stir in enough water to make a stiff dough.
2. **Knead** lightly together, until dough forms a ball. Divide dough in two pieces -- ⅓ of dough for bottom crust and ⅔ of dough for top crust. Wrap and chill well before using.
3. **Roll** bottom crust to desired size on lightly floured surface. Line pie plate with pastry; add filling; and top with second crust.

YIELD: one 10-inch deep dish crust

Carrot Chiffon Pie

*Here's a departure from the old Thanksgiving standby, "pumpkin chiffon." Great anytime of year, this recipe comes from the files of Phyllis Cline and **Forty Carrots** of Memphis, Tennessee.*

1   envelope unflavored gelatin
      softened in ¼ cup of milk
½   cup milk
½   cup sugar
½   teaspoon salt
¼   teaspoon ground cardamom
½   teaspoon ground mace
¼   teaspoon ground ginger
¼   teaspoon ground nutmeg
2   egg yolks, slightly beaten
1   cup carrots, cooked and mashed
2   egg whites
¼   cup sugar
½   cup whipping cream, whipped
1   9-inch graham-cracker crust

1. **Combine** gelatin and milk mixture with ½ cup milk in heavy saucepan and heat gently to dissolve gelatin. Remove from heat.
2. **Add** sugar, salt, cardamom, mace, ginger and nutmeg to gelatin mixture.
3. **Combine** egg yolks and carrots in a small bowl and whisk well. Add 4 tablespoons of milk mixture, 1 tablespoon at a time, to eggs and carrots. Blend in warmed egg yolks and carrots with remaining milk, sugar and spice mixture. Cook 5 minutes at very low heat, being careful not to curdle the eggs. Remove from heat and chill until partially set.
4. **Beat** egg whites until soft peaks form. Gradually add ¼ cup sugar and beat to stiff peaks. Fold into carrot mixture along with whipped cream. Pile into crust. Chill until firm.

YIELD: 6-8 servings

The Memphis Queen Line

The South's Premier Riverboat Company

Presents

Cookies
and
Candy

THE MEMPHIS QUEEN LINE STORY

The **Memphis Queen Line** was founded in 1955 by Captain Ed Langford. In 1960, Captain Tom Meanley purchased the MEMPHIS QUEEN II and began building boats in his backyard and on the banks of the Mississippi River. His son, Captain Jake Meanley, and daughter, Captain Dale Meanley Lozier, developed the operation over the next 25 years with the help of Captain Dale's husband, the late Captain John H. Lozier. Today, the **Memphis Queen Line** is into its third generation of family owners with Captain Dale's two sons, Captain John Lozier and Captain William Lozier, involved in the operation.

The **Memphis Queen Line** Riverboat Company is comprised of four vessels -- MEMPHIS QUEEN II, MEMPHIS QUEEN III, ISLAND QUEEN AND MEMPHIS SHOWBOAT -- and serves over 150,000 passengers annually on over 1,000 cruises.

Since 1955, the **Memphis Queen Line** has cruised over 30 million passenger miles on a variety of sailing trips from the historic cobblestone wharf, on the banks of the Mississippi River, in Downtown Memphis, Tennessee.

The **Memphis Queen Line** is the only local excursion passenger vessel company operating in the lower Mississippi River between St. Louis and New Orleans (1,100 miles). Passengers experience the currents of the mighty Mississippi River aboard an authentic replica of an old-time paddlewheeler. Sightseeing Cruises, Dinner Cruises and Private Party Cruises are all options. Dinner Cruises offer Marinated Chicken Breast & Barbecue or Captain's Prime Rib, full cash bar with wine list, and a live Memphis or Dixieland Band!

Riverside Drive at Monroe Ave.
Memphis, Tennessee 38103
800-221-6197 * WWW.Memphis.Queen.Com

Chocolate Cracker Candy

Quick, different and good.

35 to 40 saltine crackers
1 cup unsalted butter + 1 tablespoon for greasing pan
1 cup light brown sugar, packed
1 12-ounce package milk chocolate chips

Preheat oven to 400 degrees.

1. **Cover** cookie sheet with aluminum foil; grease foil with butter.
2. **Arrange** crackers in overlapping pattern on foil.
3. **Melt** butter in saucepan; add brown sugar, stirring until it comes to a boil. Reduce heat to low and simmer 3 minutes; remove from heat.
4. **Pour** brown sugar mixture over crackers.
5. **Bake** at 400 degrees for 5 minutes.
6. **Remove** from oven, sprinkle milk chocolate chips over cracker mixture.
7. **Cool** for 15 minutes then spread chocolate with a spatula.
8. **Cool** completely, and break into pieces.

YIELD: about 36 pieces.

Louisiana Pralines

A line of cars watched from the bank, as the ferry slowly made its way across the Mississippi River at St. Francisville, Louisiana. My husband and I were on our way to Lafayette. It was unseasonably warm for an October afternoon, making most passengers abandon their cars to catch the river breeze.

From nowhere, appeared an old black woman carrying a straw basket filled with homemade pralines for sale. Her steps were shuffled, and her skin weathered. I did not know anything about those pralines, but I admired her effort. For a dollar, two well-wrapped pralines rested in my hand. Maybe half the people had bought pralines from the old woman before she began her trip back down the dusty road.

The heat filled the air with the smell of caramel and pecans as everyone began to eat. Talk about melt-in-your-mouth good! As quickly as I could find my voice, I shouted for my husband to catch the old woman and to buy more pralines. He did, and so did every-one else! This time, as she turned to go back home, her basket was empty.

Those were the best pralines I have ever eaten, and the "inspiration" for the following recipe.

1	**cup brown sugar, packed**
1	**cup white sugar**
¼	**teaspoon salt**
¾	**cup evaporated milk**
3	**tablespoons butter**
½	**teaspoon pure vanilla extract**

1½ cups pecan pieces

1. **Mix** sugars, salt and evaporated milk in a heavy saucepan.
2. **Slowly** bring to a boil until the soft ball stage is reached on a candy thermometer, about 234 degrees. Quickly remove mixture from heat and beat until creamy.
3. **Stir** in butter, vanilla and pecans.
4. **Drop** by spoonfuls on buttered wax paper and cool. Wrap in aluminum foil and store in tightly covered containers.

YIELD: about 20 pralines

Great-Grandmother's beauty secret--Wrinkle Cream - Mix 2 tablespoons cream with 1 teaspoon honey, apply to face and throat. When dry, remove with warm water.

Tea Cake Cookies

When I eat these cookies, I become five again, sitting on the wooden bench in my Grandmother Mays' kitchen, sampling each tray as they come out of the oven. That bench and these cookies have spun a web of fond memories for four generations.

2	**cups self-rising flour**
1	**cup sugar**
¾	**cup corn oil**
1	**egg**
¼	**teaspoon pure vanilla extract**
¼	**teaspoon pure lemon extract**

Preheat oven to 350 degrees.

1. **Mix** ingredients in order given.
2. **Roll** into balls, about the size of a half-dollar.
3. **Place** 3 inches a part on cookie sheet.
4. **Flatten** cookies with bottom of heavy glass.
5. **Bake** for 6 to 8 minutes or until edges start to brown. Do not overcook.
6. **Remove** from pan. Let cool on rack.

Yield: 24 cookies

Sunflower Seed Cookies

Kansas and Nebraska made these tasty cookies famous. I tasted them for the first time, while staying in a Victorian inn, on the Missouri River, in Atchison, Kansas, birthplace of Amelia Earhart.

2   cups sugar
1½ cups unsalted butter
2¾ cups self-rising flour
½   teaspoon pure vanilla extract
1   cup shelled sunflower seeds, chopped fine or ground
½   cup pecan pieces, chopped fine or ground

Preheat oven to 350 degrees.

1.   **Mix** ingredients well, in order given. Mixture will be crumbly.
2.   **Roll** into 1½-inch balls. Place on ungreased cookie sheet and flatten with bottom of glass.
3.   **Bake** at 350 degrees for about 10 minutes, or until starting to brown. Do not overbake.

YIELD: about 36 cookies

Tea-Time Brown Sugar Goodies

*Step back in time with these old-fashioned bar cookies that **Memphis Queen Line** serves during their "High Tea Cruises." Close your eyes and you can almost feel yourself slowly drifting down Ol' Man River.*

1   cup butter
1   cup white sugar
4   eggs, separated
3   cups all-purpose flour
1   teaspoon pure vanilla extract
2   cups brown sugar
1   cup nuts, chopped
    powdered sugar, optional

Preheat the oven to 325 degrees

1. **Cream** the butter and sugar; add the egg yolks one at a time; mix well.
2. **Add** flour and vanilla to butter mixture; pat thinly on an ungreased 15 x 10-inch shallow pan.
3. **Beat** the 4 egg whites in a separate bowl until stiff. Add 2 cups brown sugar, folding in well. Spread mixture evenly over the batter in pan.
4. **Sprinkle** top with one cup chopped nuts.
5. **Bake** at 325 degrees for 30 to 35 minutes, until toothpick inserted in center comes out clean.
6. **Cool.** Cut into squares.
7. **Sprinkle** with powdered sugar, if desired.

YIELD: 2-3 dozen cookies.

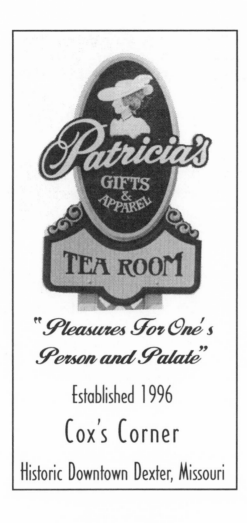

"*Pleasures For Oné s Person and Palate*"

Established 1996

Cox's Corner

Historic Downtown Dexter, Missouri

Presents

Christmas Favorites

PATRICIA'S TEA ROOM - GIFTS & APPAREL

PATRICIA'S, where pleasures can be found for one's person and palate, opened its doors in May of 1996. **PATRICIA'S Tea Room**, gift shop and boutique is located at Cox's Corner in Historical Downtown Dexter, Missouri.

Open from 10 a.m. to 6 p.m. six days a week, **PATRICIA'S** offers lunch from 11 a.m. to 2 p.m. each day with seasonal selections of outstanding salads, sandwiches and daily specials. Known for its deliciously sinful desserts and special "House Tea," the Tea Room is open for desserts until closing each day.

On the first Tuesday of each month, **PATRICIA'S** features an "American High Tea" (reservations required). Children's tea parties can be booked for all ages, with dress-up attire provided.

PATRICIA'S "Dodd Room," a Victorian-themed room, is available for catered receptions and fine dining. The country garden "Loft" is open to the community, with advance notice, for small gatherings. And, there is outdoor dining with a croquet court for the enjoyment of all.

PATRICIA'S Purple Society and the Ladies Victorian Society meet each month, providing special events for friendship and the celebration of life's experiences.

Patricia and her "Care Team" have created a shop that is fun to visit -- filled to the brim with treasures for every occasion. Come to **PATRICIA'S** early in the morning and spend the day -- you won't be disappointed.

Patricia's Tea Room - Gifts & Apparel

429 N. Walnut
Dexter, Missouri 63841
573-624-6887

Christmas Morning Strawberry Preserves

I hope that the recipe for these preserves, a Christmas morning tradition at our house, will make sweet memories for you, too. Serve with hot buttered biscuits or French toast.

1   **quart fresh or frozen whole strawberries**
1   **cup sugar**

1.   **Slice** strawberries.
2.   **Pour** sugar over strawberries, let stand 15 minutes.
3.   **Cook** in heavy saucepan over medium heat for 30 minutes.

YIELD: about 1½ cups

NOTE: I like to freeze my own berries, in summer, when they're plentiful.

Grandma "Lissa's" Snowballs

Grandma "Lissa" (Melissa Fourthman) and I share a precious bond --
our grandaughter, Ellie Potter. This is a fun-to-make holiday treat for
the three of us.

¼   **cup evaporated milk**
8   **marshmallows**

12   **marshmallows, halved**

1½ **cups shredded frozen or canned coconut**

1.   **Put** evaporated milk and 8 marshmallows in top of double
      boiler and cook over boiling water until marshmallows are
      dissolved, stirring constantly.
2.   **Remove** from heat, but keep mixture standing over hot water.
3.   **Dip** halved marshmallows into the warm mixture, one at a time
      using two forks.
4.   **Roll** in shredded coconut.
5.   **Put** on waxed paper to cool.

     YIELD: 2 dozen snowballs

Great-Great Aunt Loubell's Gingerbread or Treacle Bread

Aunt Loubell lived on a Tennessee hilltop, where she was well-known for her hand-painted Christmas decorations and her special holiday, molasses-laden gingerbread. The elder members of our family refer to this as "Treacle Bread." Treacle is the Irish word for molasses.

½   **cup butter, melted**
½   **cup sugar**
½   **cup buttermilk**
1   **cup light molasses**
2   **cups self-rising flour, sifted**
½   **teaspoon baking soda**
½   **teaspoon cinnamon**
1½ **teapsoons ginger**
1   **cup finely chopped nuts**

Preheat oven to 350 degrees.

1. **Grease** and flour a 9 x 4 x 3-inch loaf pan.
2. **Cream** butter and sugar together.
3. **Add** buttermilk and molasses, mix well.
4. **Combine** flour, baking soda and spices.
5. **Add** to molasses mixture gradually, mixing well.
6. **Stir** in nuts.
7. **Pour** into prepared loaf pan.
8. **Bake** for 50-60 minutes, or until a wooden pick inserted in center comes out clean.
9. **Cool** in pan for 15 minutes. Invert onto serving plate; top with whipped cream or ice cream, if desired.

YIELD: 8-10 servings.

Holiday Party Bon-Bon Cookies

It wouldn't be Christmas in our home without these party perfect cookies.

1	cup unsalted butter
⅓	cup powdered sugar
1¼	cups self-rising flour
¾	cup cornstarch
½	cup chopped English walnuts or pecans

1	cup powdered sugar
1	tablespoon vegetable oil
2	tablespoons fresh lemon juice
	candied cherries for garnish

Preheat oven to 350 degrees.

1. **Beat** butter and ⅓ cup powdered sugar until creamy.
2. **Sift** flour and cornstarch into butter mixture; stir well.
3. **Add** nuts.
4. **Shape** dough, 1 teaspoon at a time, into balls.
5. **Place** on cookie sheet and flatten tops slightly.
6. **Bake** at 350 degrees for 10 minutes, or until golden brown.
7. **Cool** on wire rack for 15 minutes.
8. **Blend** 1 cup powdered sugar, vegetable oil and lemon juice. Pour glaze over cookies.
9. **Place** cookies on serving dish and garnish with candied cherries.

YIELD: 18-24 cookies

Hot Spiced Fruit

This family recipe is especially good with ham or turkey.

1   16-ounce can pineapple chunks
1   16-ounce can sliced peaches
1   16-ounce can pears
1   16-ounce can apricot halves
1   cup light brown sugar, packed
½   cup butter, melted
1   teaspoon cinnamon

Preheat oven to 325 degrees.

1.   **Drain** fruits and cut into large pieces.
2.   **Combine** brown sugar, butter and cinnamon.
3.   **Add** sugar mixture to fruit.
4.   **Pour** into a 9 x 13-inch baking dish.
5.   **Bake** at 325 degrees for 1 hour.

YIELD: 8 servings

Viola's Glazed Apple Cookies

The taste of Christmas in a cookie! My 87 year-old friend, Viola, a Missouri transplant from Long Island, New York, shares this 1890's recipe she got from a dear friend many years ago.

½ **cup vegetable shortening**
1⅓ **cups dark brown sugar, packed**
½ **teaspoon salt**
½ **teaspoon ground cloves**
1 **teaspoon cinnamon**
½ **teaspoon nutmeg**
1 **egg beaten**
2 **cups flour**
1 **teaspoon baking soda**
1 **cup finely chopped, peeled apples**
½ **cup chopped raisins**
1 **cup chopped nuts**
¼ **cup apple juice or milk**

Preheat oven to 400 degrees.

1. **Cream** shortening in a bowl.
2. **Add** brown sugar, salt, cloves, cinnamon, nutmeg and egg, beating well.
3. **Combine** flour with baking soda and add ½ to creamed mixture, blending well.
4. **Stir** in fruits, nuts and apple juice or milk.
5. **Add** the remaining flour mixture and mix well.
6. **Drop** by tablespoonfuls onto greased baking sheet. Bake until lightly browned, about 11 minutes. Do not overbake.
7. **Remove** to rack, and while still hot, top with glaze (p.160).

YIELD: 48 cookies

Glaze
(Viola's Glazed Apple Cookies)

1½ cups sifted powdered sugar
1   tablespoon soft butter
¼   teaspoon vanilla extract
1½ tablespoons scalded milk

1. **Blend** all ingredients well.
2. **Glaze** cookies.
3. **Let** cookies dry before packing in tins.

*NOTE: Because of the apple, these cookies stay moist and can be stored in tins for 2-3 weeks before Christmas.

Great-Grandmother's household hint - To dry clean a shirt, put 4-ounces of cornmeal into a 24-pound flour sack and gently rub meal over all the shirt. Leave it for a day, shake and dust thoroughly, press with hot iron.

New Year's Eve Bourbon Pecan Cake

A cake that kindles memories of days gone by, when there really were sleigh bells and chestnuts roasting on an open fire!

1   cup unsalted butter
1   16-ounce box light brown sugar
6   eggs
4   cups self-rising flour
1   teaspoon nutmeg
2   teaspoons cinnamon
1   teaspoon baking soda
½   teaspoon salt
1   cup bourbon
1   15-ounce box seedless raisins, light or dark
2   pounds pecan pieces

Preheat oven to 225 degrees.

1. **Grease** a large angel food cake pan with vegetable shortening and dust it with flour.
2. **Beat** butter and sugar in large bowl, until creamy.
3. **Beat** in eggs, one at a time.
4. **Sift** flour, nutmeg, cinnamon, baking soda and salt together.
5. **Add** dry ingredients and bourbon, alternately, to creamed mixture.
6. **Stir** in raisins and pecans.
7. **Turn** cake batter into prepared angel food cake pan.
8. **Bake** at 225 degrees for 3½ hours.
9. **Cool** for 15 minutes in the pan. Remove and complete cooling on rack.

YIELD: 12-16 servings

Special Friends
&
Recipes

Carolyn Sue's Potato Dumplings

As best sidekicks, Carolyn Farrenburg and I often get into mischief. (If you have never eaten a frozen chocolate covered banana on-a-stick, you should!) Carolyn and I have fluted the edges of our lives with rollicking fun, and hearty food like these potato dumplings.

2   to 3 large baking potatoes, peeled
½   teaspoon salt, more if desired
4   tablespoons butter, more if desired

2½ cups self-rising flour
1   tablespoon water
2   eggs, beaten

1.   **Cut** potatoes in small pieces and place in large pot, cover well with water. Add salt and butter. Simmer until tender.
2.   **Mix** flour, water and eggs, while potatoes cook.
3.   **Turn** dough onto floured surface and knead until stiff, adding flour as needed to prevent sticking.
4.   **When** potatoes are done, pinch off pieces of dough (about the size of a quarter) and drop on top of simmering potatoes.
5.   **Cover** and continue to simmer for 15 minutes, or until dumplings are puffed and firm.

YIELD: 4 to 6 servings

My Apple Dumpling Friend

My rich and treasured friendship with Donna Burk began over a buttery crispy-crusted apple dumpling. Years later, our best conversations still take place over an apple dumpling and a cup of coffee.

6   **medium tart apples**
6   **tablespoons shortening**
2   **cups self-rising flour**
½   **cup cold milk**
½   **cup sugar**
2   **teaspoons cinnamon**
½   **stick softened butter**
½   **stick melted butter**

Preheat oven to 350 degrees.

1.   **Peel** and core apples, leaving apples whole.
2.   **Cut** shortening into flour.
3.   **Add** milk, mixing until you have a smooth dough. Knead dough on a floured board until smooth.
4.   **Divide** dough into 6 portions. Roll portions out big enough to cover apple.
5.   **Mix** sugar, cinnamon and softened butter.
6.   **Set** an apple on each pastry portion, put equal amounts of sugar/cinnamon mixture in each core hole.
7.   **Bring** pastry over apple, sealing by pinching together (if necessary, moisten edges).
8.   **Place** apple dumplings in a greased 9x13-inch baking dish. Brush with melted butter.
9.   **Bake** at 350 degrees for 35-40 minutes, or until golden brown.

Top with Hot Caramel Sauce (p. 171) and/or ice cream.

YIELD: 6 servings

Patty Gail's Zinger Of A Salad

At six years old I was the only grandchild, then Patsy Mays Studie was born. I always loved her as my little cousin, but as the years went by she also became my cherished friend. In life, I am the kosher dill and she is the purple onion. Zingers are our specialty.

1   **large head of iceberg lettuce, chopped**
1   **15-ounce can kidney beans, drained**
3   **hard-boiled eggs, chopped**
1   **small purple onion, thinly sliced**
1   **large carrot, shredded**
3   **kosher dill-pickle spears, diced**
½   **cup Italian dressing**
2   **tablespoons mayonnaise**
     salt and pepper to taste

1.   **Mix** all ingredients together in a 6 quart bowl.
2.   **Flavor** is best if refrigerated for at least 2 hours before serving.

YIELD: 4 to 6 servings

Great Grandmother's Beauty Secret - Oily Skin Mask - Mix 1 egg white with 1 tablespoon oatmeal, apply to face and throat for 15 minutes. Remove with warm water.

Marian's Unusual Green Tomato Pie

Marian Bock is a bright and considerate comrade, who adds tang to everyday life with this racy pie.

½ **cup sugar**
½ **teaspoon salt**
½ **teaspoon cinnamon**
2 **tablespoons quick-cooking tapioca**
1 **tablespoon lemon juice**
1 **teaspoon grated lemon peel**
6-8 green tomatoes, sliced
2 **tablespoons butter**
2 **10-inch pie crusts**

Preheat oven to 350 degrees.

1. **Mix** sugar, salt, cinnamon and tapioca.
2. **Sprinkle** bottom of pie crust with ½ of sugar mixture, and ½ of lemon juice and peel.
3. **Add** tomatoes and top with the other ½ of sugar mixture and lemon.
4. **Dot** top of filling with butter. Cover with remaining pie crust, and cut 3 or 4 small slits on top.
5. **Bake** at 350 degrees for 35-40 minutes or until golden brown.

YIELD: 8 servings

Pam's Coconut Banana Chocolate Cream Pie

A favorite confidante of mine is Pam Gard. If Pam says it's true, then it's true. So, when she says that this pie is very low-fat and really delicious -- you know that you've got to try it!

1 chocolate-flavored purchased pie crust
2 medium bananas sliced (2 cups)
1 4-serving package sugar-free instant chocolate pudding mix
⅔ cup nonfat dry milk powder
1⅓ cups water
1 cup fat-free Cool Whip
1 teaspoon coconut extract
2 tablespoons flaked coconut

1. **Layer** sliced bananas in pie crust.
2. **In** medium bowl, mix dry pudding mix and dry milk powder.
3. **Add** water and mix well, using a wire whisk.
4. **Blend** in ¼ cup Cool Whip and ½ teaspoon of coconut extract. Spread evenly over bananas.
5. **Refrigerate** while making topping.
6. **Combine** ¾ cup of Cool Whip and remaining ½ teaspoon coconut extract in a small bowl; spread mixture evenly over set pudding mixture.
7. **Sprinkle** coconut over top. Refrigerate 2 hours.

YIELD: 6 to 8 servings

Martha's Fiesta Chicken

Listen closely, and you'll hear the Mariachis playing as you dine on the fiesta of flavors in this South-of-the-Border chicken dish. My friend, Martha Hailey, says this is easy, spicy and good. Olé!

6	large chicken breasts
½	cup chicken broth
1	can cream of mushroom soup
1	can cream of chicken soup
1	can Rotel tomatoes
1	tablespoon garlic powder
	salt and pepper to taste
1	9-ounce bag Doritos, crushed
24	ounces Monterey Jack cheese, shredded

Preheat oven to 350 degrees

1. **Place** chicken in pot and cover with water. Bring to a boil, then reduce heat to simmer for 45 minutes, turning chicken occasionally, until done. Do not overcook.
2. **Skin** and de-bone the chicken; cut into cubes. Save ½ cup broth for sauce.
3. **Mix** soups, Rotel tomatoes, garlic powder, chicken broth, salt and pepper to make sauce.
4. **Grease** a 9 x 13-inch pan, and line with a layer of crushed Doritos.
5. **Add** a layer of chicken, then top with sauce and cheese.
6. **Repeat** layers, ending with cheese on top.
7. **Bake** at 350 degrees for 30 minutes.

YIELD: 4-6 servings

Lee Ann's Flavorful Chicken Tetrazzini

Lee Ann Halstead is a multi-talented artist whose graphic renditions have soul and feeling. She transformed my words into the captivating cover of this book. One of Lee Ann's best culinary renditions is her Chicken Tetrazzini.

1	6-pound chicken (or hen)
1	pound thin spaghetti
1	stick butter
2	green peppers
4	tablespoons flour
2	cups milk
2	cups mushrooms, sliced
1	teaspoon garlic powder
2	teaspoons fresh garlic, chopped
1	tablespoon Worcestershire sauce
2	small jars diced pimentos
½	cup sherry
4	cups grated cheddar cheese (save ½ cup for topping)
¾	cup parmesan cheese

1. **Boil**, skin and de-bone chicken. Cut into bite-size pieces and reserve.
2. **Cook** spaghetti in chicken broth (add water if needed). Drain. (While spaghetti is cooking, preheat oven to 350 degrees.)
3. **Sauté** peppers in butter, in large dutch oven, until transparent; add flour and brown lightly.

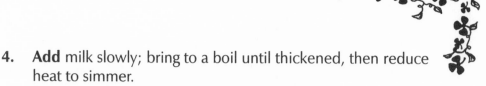
4. **Add** milk slowly; bring to a boil until thickened, then reduce heat to simmer.

5. **Add** mushrooms, garlic powder, chopped garlic, Worcestershire sauce, pimentos and reserved chicken.

6. **Stir** in sherry, 3½ cups of the grated cheddar cheese and parmesan cheese. Toss with cooked spaghetti.

7. **Place** Chicken Tetrazzini in a large greased casserole dish. Top with remaining ½ cup grated cheddar cheese.

8. **Cover** and bake at 350 degrees for 20 minutes; uncover and continue baking for 10 minutes more, or until lightly browned.

YIELD: 6 servings

Gina's Poppy Seed Bread

A saucy lady with a heart of gold, that's Gina Shell. She's added more than a little flavor to my life over the years. This is Gina's favorite and "only" recipe.

3   cups all-purpose flour
1½ teaspoons baking powder
1½ teaspoons salt
2¼ cups sugar
3   eggs
1½ cups milk
1½ cups oil
2   tablespoons poppy seeds
2   teaspoons pure vanilla extract
2   teaspoons butter flavoring

Preheat the oven to 350 degrees.

1. **Mix** together all ingredients in order given.
2. **Beat** 2 minutes.
3. **Pour** batter into lightly greased loaf pans.*
4. **Bake** for 1 hour at 350 degrees.
5. **Pour** Poppy Seed Glaze (p. 171) over hot bread.

YIELD: *three 9 x 5-inch loaf pans or 5 "mini" loaf pans.

Mary Sue's Gumdrop Cake

Mary Sue Hicks and I are like gracefully-seasoned Mississippi River willow trees-- that may bend in the wind, but always spring back poised. When Mary Sue springs back, she always makes something delicious to eat, like this jolly-good Gumdrop Cake.

4	cups self-rising flour
1	teaspoon cinnamon
½	teaspoon cloves
½	teaspoon nutmeg
½	teaspoon salt
1	cup gumdrops, diced (any flavor)
1	cup white raisins
1	cup chopped nuts
2	cups sugar
1	cup shortening
2	eggs
1½	cups applesauce
1	teaspoon pure vanilla extract
1	teaspoon baking soda, dissolved in 1 tablespoon hot water

Preheat oven to 325 degrees.

1. **Sift** flour, spices and salt together; use small portion to dredge gumdrops, raisins and nuts.
2. **Cream** shortening and sugar. Add eggs one at a time.
3. **Blend** in applesauce. Add dry ingredients.
4. **Stir** in vanilla and baking soda. Fold in gumdrops, raisins and nuts.
5. **Pour** into 2 large well-greased and floured loaf pans.
6. **Bake** 2 hours at 325 degrees or until a knife inserted in center comes out clean. Remove from oven. Let cool in pans for 15 minutes.
7. **Wrap** in aluminum foil and store in refrigerator until ready to serve or they can be frozen**.**

YIELD: 2 9 x 5-inch loaves

Old-Time Apple Butter

Criss-crossed lives have given Sharon Medlin and me a friendship like her great-grandmother's old-time apple butter--good to the last jar.

Sharon's great-grandmother gave her this recipe when she was married in the late 1960's, with the hope that Sharon would get a smile from it. Now, we share the recipe -- and the smile -- with you.

1. **Boil** one barrel of new cider down to half the orginal.
2. **Peel** and core three bushels of cooking apples; add to boiled-down cider.
3. **Stir** constantly for 8 to 10 hours -- will adhere to inverted plate.
4. **Put** away in stone jars (not earthenware) covering first with writing paper cut to fit jar - press closely upon the apple butter; and then cover the whole with thick brown paper.
5. **Tie** down, snugly!

If you don't have a barrel of apple cider - or stone jars! - here is the **APPLE BUTTER** recipe for you.

2   **cups sugar (white or brown)**
1   **teaspoon cinnamon**
½   **teaspoon cloves**
¼   **teaspoon allspice**
2   **cups apple cider or water**
4   **pounds tart apples**
    juice of one lemon

1. **Heat** sugar, cinnamon, cloves, allspice and cider or water until sugar dissolves.
2. **Add** to sugar liquid peeled, cored and sliced apples, plus lemon juice.
3. **Simmer** uncovered until mixture is thickened, about 1¼ hours, stirring frequently.
4. **Turn** into sterilized jars and seal.

YIELD: about 5 pints.

Hot Caramel Sauce

1   **stick butter**
1   **cup light brown sugar**
½   **cup heavy cream**
½   **teapsoon pure vanilla extract**

1.   **Combine** butter, sugar and cream in small saucepan. Cook stirring, over medium heat until thickened.
2.   **Stir** in vanilla extract. Serve with **Apple Dumpling** (p.161)

   YIELD: 1½ cups

Glaze For Poppy Seed Bread

¾   **cup powdered sugar**
¼   **cup orange juice**
1½ **teaspoons pure vanilla extract**
2   **teaspoons butter flavoring**

1.   **Mix** together and pour over hot bread.
2.   **Let** stand 30 minutes. Remove bread from pans. Serve with **Gina's Poppy Seed Bread** (p. 168).

Hot Buttered Apple Cider

This warming concoction will perk up spirits and kindle friendships.

¼   **pound softened butter**
½   **teaspoon powdered cloves**
½   **teaspoon ground cinnamon**
½   **teaspoon nutmeg**
1   **16-ounce box light brown sugar**
6   **ounces apple cider per serving**

1.   **Mix** butter, spices and brown sugar very well. Put in refrigerator until needed.
2.   **Heat** cider in tea kettle. Put 1 tablespoon butter mixture in each cup and fill with hot cider. Stir well.

YIELD: 12 servings

Index

Index

ORDER COPIES OF

DROP DUMPLIN'S AND PAN-FRIED MEMORIES...
Along the Mississippi
By Angie Thompson Holtzhouser

from

FAYJOE ENTERPRISES
P.O. BOX 10
LILBOURN, Missouri 63862

Enclosed is my check or money order, made payable to:

FAYJOE ENTERPRISES.

Price per Book	$ 14.95
Tax per Book	.86
Shipping & Handling per Book	3.75
Total Cost Per Book	$ 19.56

TOTAL NUMBER OF BOOKS ORDERED _____

TOTAL AMOUNT ENCLOSED $ _____

NAME

_____

ADDRESS _____

CITY _____ STATE _____ ZIP _____

PLEASE ALLOW 4 TO 6 WEEKS FOR DELIVERY

REMEMBER -- COOKBOOKS MAKE GREAT GIFTS!